D1794886

AN ENTERPRISE MAP OF GHANA

AN ENTERPRISE MAP OF GHANA

John Sutton and Bennet Kpentey

FSC
www.fsc.org
MIX
Paper from
responsible sources
FSC® C020438

CONTENTS

ABOUT THE AUTHORS

John Sutton is the Sir John Hicks Professor of Economics at the London School of Economics.

Bennet Kpentey is the Chief Executive of Sync Consult Limited, a management and financial consulting firm in Accra, Ghana. He is also a part-time lecturer in Strategic Management at the University of Ghana Business School on the Executive MBA Programme.

The International Growth Centre (www.theigc.org) promotes sustainable growth in developing countries by providing demand-led policy advice based on frontier research. The IGC is directed and organized from hubs at the London School of Economics and the University of Oxford and comprises country offices across the developing world. The IGC was initiated and is funded by the Department for International Development (DFID).

John Sutton's Enterprise Map Project aims to provide a standardized descriptive account of the industrial capabilities of selected countries in sub-Saharan Africa. This is the second volume to appear.

ACKNOWLEDGEMENTS

The authors express their appreciation to all the organizations, firms and individuals who supported this work in diverse ways. Special appreciation is accorded to the representatives who devoted time to meeting the research team to make the participation of their firms in this Enterprise Map possible.

The authors also thank Hanna Tetteh, Minister of Trade and Industry, Nii Ansah-Adjaye, Chief Director at the Ministry of Trade and Industry, Seth Twum-Akwaboah, the Executive Director of the Association of Ghana Industries (AGI), and Dr Sam Mensah, the Country Director of IGC Ghana, for the immense support they provided in facilitating the research process and engagement with the firms. We also thank Ghana Statistical Service, the Ghana Export Promotion Council, the Ghana Investment Promotion Centre and various data sources in Ghana for providing the necessary information and data.

Finally, the Sync Consult Research team – senior consultants Angela Allotey and Walter Kpentey and the analysts – played a key role in working with the firms we profiled.

ACRONYMS AND ABBREVIATIONS

ACP	African Concrete Products Limited
ADM	Archer Daniels Midland Company
AGOA	African Growth and Opportunity Act
AOMIL	Ayiem Oil Mills Limited
ATL	Akosombo Textiles Limited
BOPP	Benso Oil Palm Plantation
BVB	Bas van Buuren
CEPS	Customs, Excise and Preventive Service
CMC	Cocoa Marketing Company
ECOWAS	Economic Community of West African States
EU	European Union
FDI	Foreign Direct Investment
FFBs	Fresh fruit bunches
GCMC	Ghana Cylinder Manufacturing Company Limited
GDP	Gross Domestic Product
GFTN	Global Forest and Trade Network
GHACEM	Ghana Cement Works Limited
GIHOC	Ghana Industrial Holding Corporation
GNPA	Ghana National Procurement Agency
GOPDC	Ghana Oil Palm Development Company
GREL	Ghana Rubber Estates Limited
GSA	Ghana Standards Authority
GTP	Ghana Textile Printing Company Limited
HDPE	High-density polyethylene
ISO	International Organization for Standardization
KACC	Kaiser Aluminum & Chemical Corporation
mt	Metric tonne
NORPALM	Norwegian Palm Ghana Limited
PSI	Presidential Special Initiative
PVC	Polyvinyl chloride
SMEs	Small and medium-sized enterprises
SSNIT	Social Security and National Insurance Trust
TOPP	Twifo Oil Palm Plantation

UAC   United Africa Company of Gold Coast
UAE   United Arab Emirates
UK   United Kingdom
UNIDO   United Nations Industrial Development Organization
uPVC   Unplasticized polyvinyl chloride
US   United States

VALCO   Volta Aluminum Company

WAM   West African Mills
WAMCO   West African Mills Company

AN ENTERPRISE MAP OF GHANA

Chapter 1

INTRODUCTION

Ghana has been one of Africa's fastest growing economies over the past decade. Between 2000 and 2009, gross domestic product (GDP) per capita rose by 63%.[1] If the growth rates of the past decade are projected forward, the much-discussed aim of Ghana becoming a middle-income country in the fairly near future looks plausible. The recent discoveries of oil make this goal seem even more achievable. But if such growth rates are to be maintained, Ghana will almost certainly need to undergo a major advance in terms of its industrial capabilities. The best point of departure to see what is needed is to ask what Ghana's current industrial capabilities are and where those capabilities came from.

The Origin of Ghana's Current Industrial Capabilities

This book describes the history and current capabilities of Ghana's leading industrial companies (agribusiness, manufacturing and construction). It surveys each of the country's major industries, and identifies the different clusters of firms engaged within each industry. Finally, it profiles 50 leading companies in depth. These 50 companies have been chosen to represent most or all of the largest firms within each segment of each industry. Taken together, these profiles provide a good picture of the current level of Ghana's industrial capabilities.

A central role in Ghana's industrial sector is played by quite a small number of leading companies. To see this, it is useful to look at the top firms in each of the main exporting industries. As Figure 1.1 shows, some 83% of Ghana's exports come from three primary-sector industries: gold, cocoa and bauxite. Of the remaining 17%, well over half comes from five industries: metal and metal products; wood and wood products; plastics and rubber; fats and oils; and the pharmaceuticals, cosmetics and related

---

[1] GDP in real US dollars, to base year 2005, rose from 7.64 billion in 2000 to 12.46 billion in 2009. Source: National Accounts Estimates of Main Aggregates, United Nations Statistics Division.

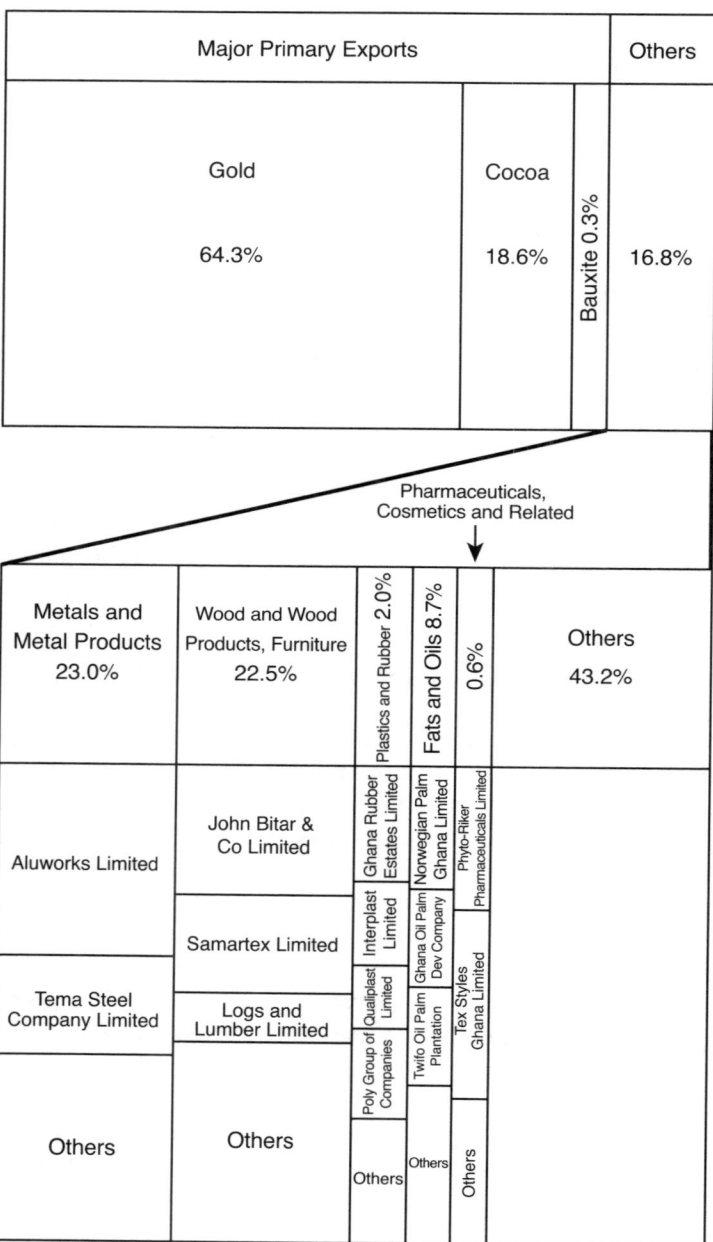

FIGURE 1.1. An export map.

group. These top eight exporting industries account for over nine-tenths of Ghana's exports.

So who are the top exporting firms? Twenty-seven firms account between them for more than half of total exports in every one of these top eight exporting industries.[2] Together, these 27 firms account for 62% of Ghana's exports.

Were we to focus on total production, rather than exports, the pattern would be similar, but reliable figures are much more difficult to pin down. The same picture still holds though: a relatively modest number of major players dominate the industrial landscape. Understanding the origin and development of the capabilities of this small group of leading firms is a natural point of departure in exploring how Ghana's industrial capabilities might be extended over the next decade.

So where do the capabilities of these leading firms come from? Of the 50 firms profiled below, just over half had their origin in the domestic private sector. (Some 23 were set up by foreign firms and/or the government of Ghana.) Of the 27 domestic private-sector firms, only 15 began life as startups in manufacturing or construction. Just under half of the 27 were offshoots of local trading companies that had been in operation for many years before venturing into manufacturing (Figure 1.2). Some examples follow below.

- Kwabena Adjare Danquah, who founded the roofing materials manufacturer Metalex Ghana Limited, had a retail business as a stockist for a major roofing materials company before setting up his own manufacturing business.
- Dr Michael Agyekum Addo was an importer of pharmaceutical products prior to setting up his manufacturing business as part of Kama Health Services Limited.
- Parlays Ghana Limited, one of Ghana's leading biscuit makers, was founded by Komla A. Hukportie, whose first business venture involved trading and distribution of foodstuffs.
- Samuel Mensah Stone spent 10 years as a supplier of aggregates to the construction industry before setting up Prime Stone Quarries.

---

[2] Five firms account for over 70% of gold production and exports: AngloGold Ashanti, Newmont Ghana, Gold Fields Ghana, Chirano Goldmines and Golden Star. Seven firms account for 85% of cocoa production and exports: Cocoa Processing Company Limited, West African Mills Company, Barry Callebaut Ghana Limited, ADM Cocoa (Ghana) Limited, Cargill Ghana Limited, Plot Enterprise Ghana Limited and Cadbury–Kraft Ghana Limited. One company, the Volta Aluminum Company, accounts for all exports of bauxite/alumina.

A further 14 firms, shown in Figure 1.1, together account for half of exports in each of the remaining five industries.

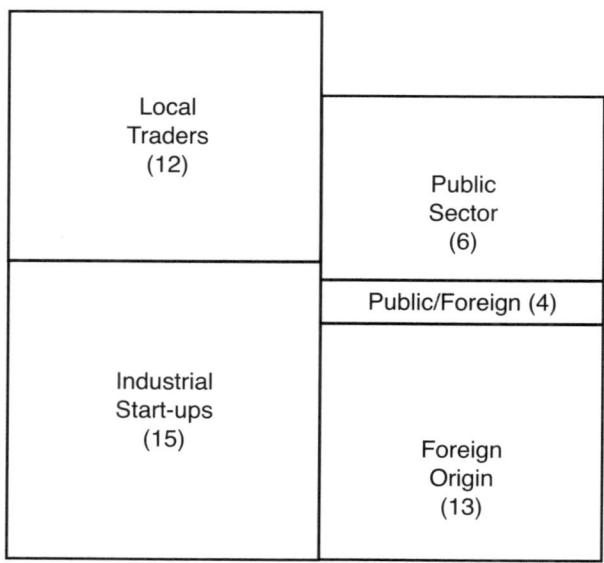

FIGURE 1.2. Origins of Ghana's leading industrial companies.

- Kwame Ofosu Bamfo had a trading business in paints before establishing Bamson Company Limited, one of Ghana's leading manufacturers of paints.

The role of trading companies as a seedbed of industrial development is a theme discussed elsewhere in this series.[3] Such companies enjoy a key advantage in terms of relevant capabilities, in that they have a deep understanding of the local market and of domestic and international supply chains that allows them to better identify viable opportunities and to source supplies effectively. Manufacturing know-how, in the basic industrial areas that most of these firms are involved in, is less difficult to acquire than this understanding and judgement of local and international markets and the organizational capital embedded in an effectively run company.[4] Moreover, these firms have access to internal finance from their

[3] Sutton, J., and N. Kellow. 2010. *An Enterprise Map of Ethiopia.* London: International Growth Centre.

[4] This point is nicely illustrated by the history of Aquafresh (Chapter 6). The company began life as a manufacturing concern in a technically unrelated industry (textiles), but on running into financial difficulties switched direction and established a new business in soft drinks. Having an effective and well-functioning organization is a key asset. Even if adverse market conditions force the firm to exit its original market, its organizational capital remains valuable in other markets.

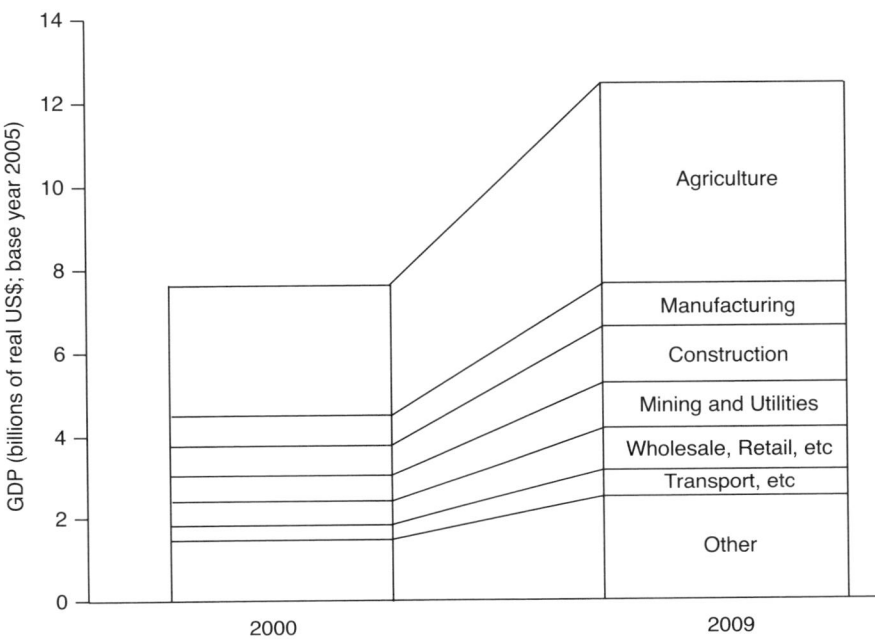

FIGURE 1.3. The change in size and composition of Ghana's GDP in real US dollars 1993–2009. ('Wholesale, retail, etc' covers wholesale, retail trade, restaurants and hotels. 'Transport, etc' covers transport, storage and communication.)

trading activities. It is for these reasons that the domestic trading sector, which is often poorly regarded as a contributor to economic growth, can in fact be a crucial seedbed for the takeoff of industrial activity.

The Sources of Growth

The figures for Ghana's overall growth record over the past decades are impressive, but the breakdown of these figures reveals an interesting picture (Figure 1.3).

The sectors that grew fastest over the nine-year period from 2000 to 2009 were construction (88%), transport, storage and communications (83%) and wholesale, retail, hotels and restaurants (81%). Mining and utilities combined grew by 70% over the period, and agriculture by 53%. The slowest growing sector was manufacturing, whose contribution to value added in real US dollars grew by 39% over this period.

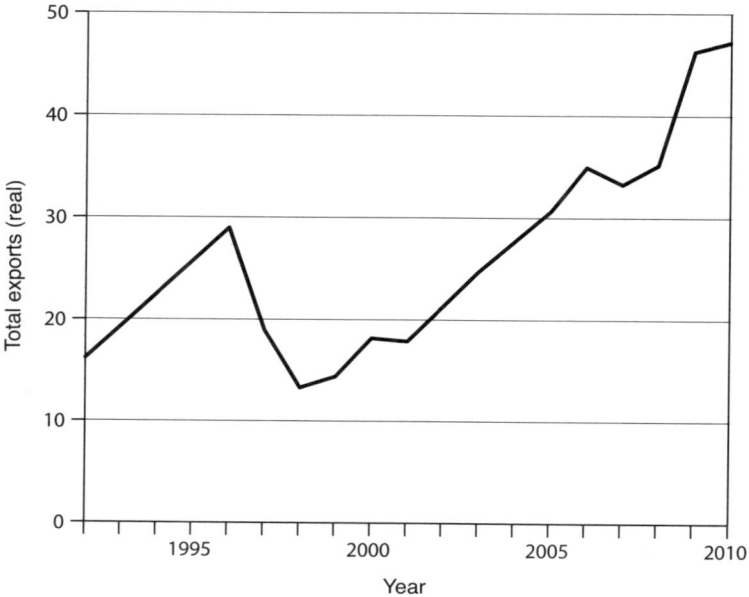

FIGURE 1.4. Total exports in real US dollars 1992–2010.

A similar picture emerges when we look at exports (Figures 1.4 and 1.5). The real US dollar value of exports rose by 193% between 1992 and 2010, with gold and cocoa accounting for 91% of the increase. Substantial investments in the gold-mining sector together with rising world prices led to a 343% rise in the real US dollar value of gold exports between 1992 and 2010. Reforms in the cocoa sector included a new price regime for farmers and a restructuring of production; the real US dollar value of exports rose by 122% over the period.[5,6] Manufacturing, on the other hand, accounted for only 8% of the rise in the real value of exports.[7]

The question raised by these observations is: can the rates of growth of the past decade be sustained on the basis of a similar profile of contributions by sector? The answer, almost certainly, is no. The reforms of the past decade in gold and cocoa have led to a major rise in the level of their respective

[5] Easterling, T., J. W. Fox and F. B. Sands. 2008. *Factors Affecting Economic Growth in Ghana: Bases for a New USAID Approach to Economic Growth.* Sibley International for USAID.

[6] Berry, L. B. (ed.) 1994. *Ghana: A Country Study.* Washington, DC: GPO for the Library of Congress.

[7] Wood manufactures (including furniture), as defined by the SITC two-digit codes 63 and 82, account for just over a quarter of the increase in manufacturing exports.

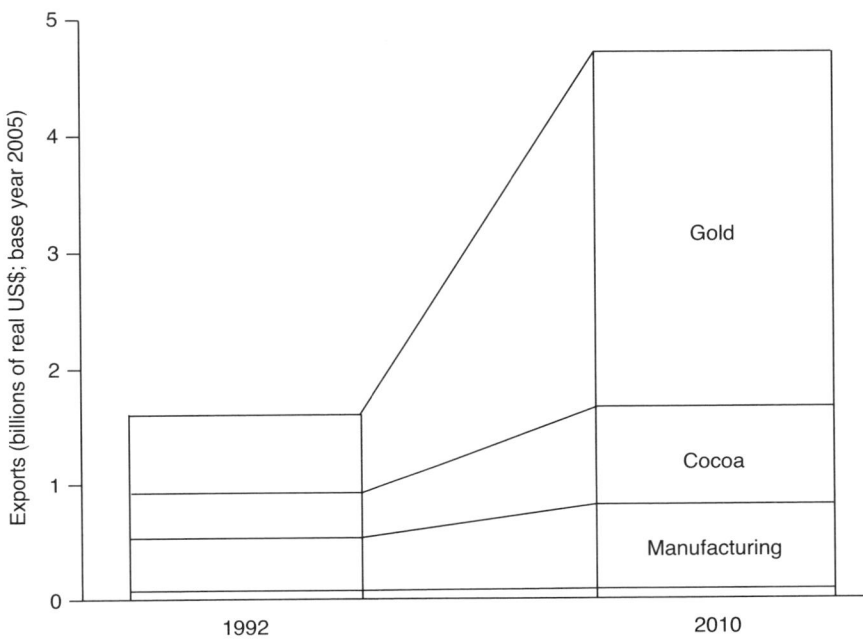

FIGURE 1.5. The change in size and composition of
Ghana's exports in real US dollars 1992–2010.

contributions. But if the growth record of the past decade is to be sustained,
it will almost certainly rest on both new contributions from the oil sector
and a substantial advance in the capabilities of the industrial sector. These
two potential sources of new growth may be quite closely intertwined.

Oil, Industry and Foreign Direct Investment (FDI)

Any major advance in Ghana's industrial capabilities beyond their present
level is likely to rest, to a substantial degree, on attracting new foreign manufacturing enterprises and integrating them effectively into the domestic
economy. Yet the record of attracting FDI over the past decade has been
disappointing for Ghana, as it has been for all countries in sub-Saharan
Africa (Table 1.1).

During the three-year period 2008–10, there were 994 new FDI projects
of which 165 were in manufacturing (Table 1.2). These projects came from
a total of 25 countries (see Tables 1.3 and 1.4). China and India together

TABLE 1.1. FDI flows and FDI stock for Ghana, selected years.

	2008	2009	2010
FDI flow (millions of US$)	1,220	1,685	2,527
$\dfrac{\text{FDI flow}}{\text{Gross fixed capital formation}}$	21.00%	37.40%	42.10%
$\dfrac{\text{FDI stock}}{\text{GDP}}$	30.20%	44.00%	51.10%

Source: UNCTAD, World Investment Report 2011 (www.unctad.org/wir or www.unctad.org/fdistatistics).

TABLE 1.2. FDI flows for the three-year period
January 2008–December 2010 by industry.

Sectors	Projects	Value (millions of US$)	Percentage of total value
Agriculture	49	514	7.4
Manufacturing	165	391	5.7
Building and construction	75	2,330	33.6
General trading	224	974	14
Export trade	55	42	0.6
Service	329	2,439	35.2
Liaison	27	30	0.4
Tourism	70	210	3.0
Total	994	6,933	100

account for 45% of new projects in this period, but the leading sources in terms of the value of projects over the period were the United Arab Emirates (UAE), Nigeria and the Netherlands.

It has been noted by observers of FDI trends that Ghana's efforts to stimulate FDI flows through improvements in the institutions charged with attracting foreign investors have not as yet made the progress that is needed.[8] The new factor of interest in this situation relates to the development of oil resources over the next few years. Oil resources always attract FDI, but in many instances the new arrivals remain semi-detached from the domestic economy. Policy instruments that require a minimum percentage of 'local content' may result in an inefficient and unhelpful multiplication of ancillary activities (such as the use of fleets of cars hired from local

[8] Easterling, T., J. W. Fox and F. B. Sands. 2008. *Factors Affecting Economic Growth in Ghana: Bases for a New USAID Approach to Economic Growth.* Sibley International for USAID.

TABLE 1.3. Number of new FDI projects in the three-year period
January 2008–December 2010 by country of origin.

Country	Registered projects
China	167
India	129
Nigeria	91
Lebanon	83
UK	57
US	40
South Africa	17
France	16
Netherlands	14
British Virgin Islands	13
Mauritius	13
Italy	11
Others (13 countries)	30
Total	681

The table shows all countries of origin that accounted for more than ten new projects over the three-year period.

TABLE 1.4. Total value of new FDI projects in the three-year period
January 2008–December 2010 by country of origin.

Country	Value of projects (millions of US$)
UAE	2,119
Nigeria	1,379
The Netherlands	1,321
Bermuda	300
Belgium/South Africa	173
Trinidad and Tobago	169
UK	167
China	127
US	123
South Africa	119
India	108
Others (combined total)	323
Total	6,429

The table shows all countries of origin accounting for more than US$100 million of inflows over the three-year period.

taxicab operators). Meanwhile, it can be the case that all fabrication work is undertaken by international subcontractors, with domestic firms playing no role. Often, this outcome is understandable, since the existing level of domestic industrial capabilities in some oil-producing (or mineral-rich) countries may be vestigial. But in Ghana this is not the case. Chapter 12 describes the current level of capabilities in the metal, engineering and assembly area. While there are no more than a handful of firms capable of large-scale metal fabrication, the opportunities for joint ventures with other firms from West Africa and elsewhere to undertake substantial projects are evident. Indeed, as we note in Chapter 12, at least one domestic firm is already active in developing appropriate joint ventures.

The opportunities for taking advantage of the development of the oil sector to advance the capabilities of domestic industrial enterprises are evident. Yet policies in this area will need to be carefully crafted if pitfalls are to be avoided. This is one of the most crucial areas meriting attention from government at the present juncture.

A Caveat

A remark is in order, regarding the descriptive statistics presented above: the 50 large and medium-sized firms profiled here are not a random sample from some larger population and nor do they comprise all industrial companies above a certain size. Rather, they comprise most or all of the leading firms within each major segment of their respective industries. This said, the set of firms profiled is not comprehensive; it did not prove possible to access the appropriate information on all leading firms.

This remark notwithstanding, it is fair to say that the profiled firms, taken together, provide a reasonably full and accurate picture of Ghana's leading enterprises across this group of industries.

Chapter 2

COCOA PROCESSING

2.1 Sector Profile

Background and overview. The cocoa industry accounts for about 3.4% of Ghana's GDP and 28%[1] of exports. It offers direct and indirect employment to two million people. Ghana is currently the second largest cocoa-producing country in the world.[2] Total production for 2011 exceeded one million metric tonnes by the end of September (Table 2.1).

Only 30% of total volume produced is processed locally, with the remaining 70% exported as raw beans to Europe, the US and Asia.

Structure of the industry. Ghana's cocoa industry comprises three segments: production, processing and marketing. Between production and processing there are activities such as drying, collection and bagging, quality control, haulage and warehousing.

Cocoa is grown in six regions: the Ashanti, Western, Central, Volta, Brong Ahafo and Eastern regions. Six large companies are involved in processing raw cocoa beans into semi-finished and finished products. Located in the Western, Ashanti and Greater Accra regions, they have a combined processing capacity of 200,000 mt per annum.

A total of 25 private, public and foreign firms are authorized by the government as Licensed Buying Companies to purchase cocoa beans from farmers on behalf of the Cocoa Marketing Company (CMC), which was established to develop and facilitate the production, processing and marketing of Ghana's cocoa.

Supply and marketing chain. Once the cocoa fruit is harvested, the beans are manually removed and then allowed to undergo fermentation before drying in the sun to reduce moisture content. After drying, they are sorted, checked for quality, bagged and transported to warehouses for delivery to

---

[1] IDPS Department, Bank of Ghana. 2011 (February). *Statistical Bulletin of the Bank of Ghana.*
[2] ICCO Quarterly Bulletin of Cocoa Statistics, Volume XXXVII, No. 2, Cocoa year 2010/11.

TABLE 2.1. Production of cocoa beans by volume, 2003–11.

Crop year	Production (mt)
2003/04	736,600
2004/05	601,900
2005/06	740,400
2006/07	614,500
2007/08	680,800
2008/09	710,600
2009/10	632,000
2010/11 (to September)	1,010,000

Source: COCOBOD/ICCO Quarterly Bulletin Report, Volume XXXVII, No. 3.

local processing facilities or for export. A summary of the supply chain is presented in Figure 2.1.

Policy context. The government aims to support the sector to increase production and expand local processing capacity through increased private-sector investment. Interventions and measures that are being implemented include supporting producer prices, providing effective disease and pest control, offering bonus payments, improving farming techniques and replanting denuded areas.

Challenges. Inadequate local processing capacity is a major problem. Meanwhile, long-term demand is threatened by the use of synthetic substitutes and cocoa extenders.

In the short term, the industry faces the inevitable difficulties posed by fluctuating prices on world markets. It also faces problems posed by smuggling of cocoa beans to neighbouring countries in response to price differentials.

Competitiveness. Ghana's cocoa beans are of high quality and attract a premium price on the world market. This reflects low levels of debris and bean defects, and an appropriate level of moisture in the beans.

The Licensed Buying Companies have buying points at the 2,700 cocoa buying stations in the cocoa growing areas. There is strong competition among the buyers, who compete by offering farmers prompt cash payment and support services including subsidized fertilizer and credit.

Ghana's semi-processed products such as cocoa liquor, cocoa butter and cocoa cake are competitively priced on the world market. However, the industry is not competitive in the market for finished products, and

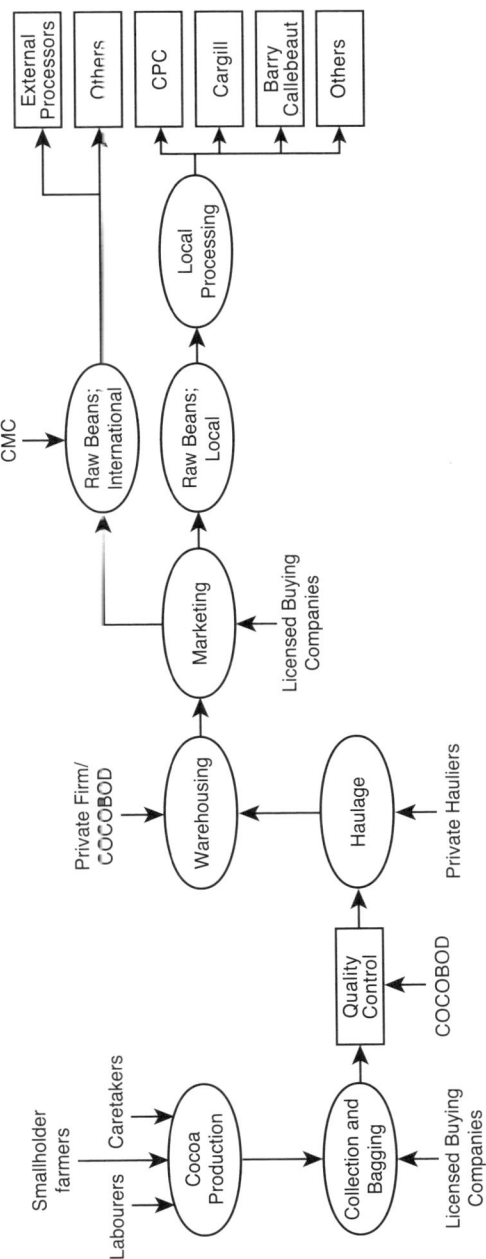

FIGURE 2.1. The cocoa supply chain.

TABLE 2.2. Export volume and value of cocoa beans and cocoa products, 2005–9.

	Cocoa beans		Cocoa product	
	Volume (thousands of mt)	Value (millions of US$)	Volume (thousands of mt)	Value (millions of US$)
2005	537	819	42.9	89.9
2006	657	1,041	78.7	146.4
2007	547	976	75.5	157
2008	564	1,225	83.9	262
2009	508	1,422	125.7	443.6

Source: Bank of Ghana (2009).

the biggest challenge is to move into exporting finished products to the international market.

Export status, strength and potential. On average, about 70% of the cocoa beans produced in Ghana are sold on the international commodity market. Export earnings from cocoa beans increased from US$819 million in 2005 to US$1.42 billion in 2009 (Table 2.2).[3]

Besides cocoa beans, Ghana exports cocoa products including chocolate and cocoa product sweets, cocoa powder, cocoa butter, cocoa liquor, cocoa cake and cocoa waste. On average, cocoa liquor accounts for 23% of total export volume. The main export destinations for cocoa liquor are the EU and the US. Cocoa cake and cocoa butter are the main processed products, accounting for 22% and 18%, respectively, of exported processed products. About 90% of the cocoa butter is exported to the Netherlands, the UK, France and the US, while 75% of cocoa cake is exported to Spain, the US and Germany.

Cocoa powder is exported mainly to Africa (Togo), the EU and the Americas. Cocoa waste is exported mainly to the Netherlands, China, Spain and Canada, while the main markets for chocolate products are Morocco, Ivory Coast, Nigeria and the UK. Total receipts from the export of cocoa products are currently in excess of US$100 million.[4]

Recent developments. In the last five years, two new cocoa processing facilities have been set up by two of the leading international cocoa companies: Cargill Incorporated and ADM Cocoa (Ghana) Limited. A new

---

[3] Analysis of data from *Statistical Bulletin of the Bank of Ghana* (February 2011; published by the IDPS Department).

[4] Export data comes from the Ghana Export Promotion Council.

local company, Plot Enterprise Ghana Limited, with a processing capacity of 32,000 mt per annum was opened in Takoradi in the Western region in early 2011 to process cocoa into liquor, butter and cake. The development of these new facilities will allow a substantial increase in the fraction of beans that are processed locally.

Current initiatives in the control of diseases and pests, improvements in soil fertility through the application of fertilization and the payment of improved producer prices to farmers[5] are expected to lead to further increases in production in the future.

Profile and line of business of large and medium-sized firms.

Real Products Limited is a Free Zones company that will come into full operation in March 2012. It is profiled in the next section.

Cocoa Processing Company Limited is a limited liability company incorporated in 1981 to process cocoa beans. Based in Tema, it has two major factories. The cocoa factory processes raw cocoa beans into semi-finished products including cocoa liquor, butter and natural/alkalized cake or powder, while the confectionery factory manufactures finished products such as chocolate bars, couverture, pebbles (chocolate coated peanuts), drinking chocolate powder, chocolate spread and natural cocoa powder.

The company increased its installed capacity from 25,000 mt per annum to 64,500 mt per annum in 2009.

West African Mills Company (WAMCO), formerly known as WAM (West African Mills), was founded by Gill and Duffus in 1947. It became a subsidiary of the Cocoa Board in 1982. WAMCO is now a joint venture between the Ghana Cocoa Board and Schroeder (part of the Hosta group of companies in Germany). The company, with an installed capacity of 75,000 mt per annum, is located in Takoradi in the Western region. The company has three factories: an expeller plant, a cocoa liquor plant and a hydraulic press plant.

WAMCO processes raw beans into cocoa butter, cocoa liquor and cocoa beans. The total volume of cocoa beans processed by the company per annum is about 50,000 mt.

The total workforce of the company is about 450.

Barry Callebaut Ghana Limited is a Free Zones enterprise located in the Tema Free Zones enclave. The headquarters of the company is in Switzerland. The company was incorporated in August 1998 to process

[5] Ministry of Finance and Economic Planning, Ghana, Budget Statement 2011.

cocoa beans into roasted nibs and cocoa liquor. The Tema factory was inaugurated in November 2001 and has an installed capacity of 60,000 mt. All cocoa beans processed by the company are sourced locally. With over 150 years' experience in the sector, the company has a global network with production sites in Europe, Africa, North and Latin America and in the Asia–Pacific region.

The company's main markets are France, Belgium, Italy, Poland, Switzerland, the US, Canada and Asia.

Cargill Incorporated, profiled in the next section, is a US-based private company that has been operating in the cocoa processing business for over 100 years. Cargill started operations in Ghana in 2007 with a factory located within the Tema Free Zones enclave.

Cadbury is a UK-based multinational. It is profiled in the next section.

Plot Enterprise Ghana Limited is a Ghanaian-owned business that came into full operation in 2010. It is profiled in the next section.

ADM Cocoa (Ghana) Limited is one of the world's largest cocoa and chocolate manufacturers. Headquartered in Illinois in the US, the company has cocoa processing plants in Europe, Africa, North America, South America, the US and Asia.

Its operations in West Africa began about 15 years ago. The company has facilities in Abidjan, Ivory Coast and a joint venture in Douala, Cameroon. ADM began operating in Ghana in 2005 and its 100,000 mt per annum cocoa processing plant was opened in Kumasi in the Ashanti region in 2009. The factory supplies semi-finished products to customers in the candy, bakery and cosmetics industries across the globe.

ADM has an estimated total workforce of 100 employees.

Afrotropic Cocoa Processing Limited is a Ghanaian-owned limited liability company. A Free Zones enterprise, it is located off the Spintex road about 15 km from the Central Business District in Accra. The company employs 90 permanent workers and has a turnover of US$12 million.

Afrotropic Cocoa Processing is a subsidiary of J. Monta and Sons Limited, a limited liability Ghanaian company established by J. Monta, an Italian, in 1924. The company has two divisions; construction and coffee. The construction division has undertaken various projects for the government of Ghana: Kumasi Airport, Kwame Nkrumah University of Science and Technology, Accra Academy School and others. The coffee division was formerly involved in exporting coffee beans to Europe, but in 2005, Afrotropic Cocoa Processing was established to add value through processing. The company has state-of-the-art equipment acquired from Italy and Germany and processes about 10,000 mt of cocoa beans annually. The company has a fully equipped laboratory. It produces pure prime pressed cocoa butter/kibble, alkalized pure prime pressed cocoa cake/kibble, natural cocoa powder, alkalized cocoa powder, dark alkalized cocoa powder and flavoured cocoa powder.

The company has adopted the ISO standards for company management and operational procedures and produces products according to ISO 22000:2005. The company is registered with the US Food and Drugs Administration and has valid certificates from that organization. Its products are kosher certified by Badatz Igud Rabbonim. The company is registered with the Islamic Food and Nutrition Council of America (IFANCA) and has a valid IFANCA halal certificate.

The company exports to the US, the Netherlands, France, Spain, the UK, Bulgaria, Hungary, the Ukraine, Iran, China, Thailand, Singapore and the Philippines.

Other processing companies. There are several small-scale cocoa processing companies in the country. These include CPI, Omanhene Cocoa Bean Company and Kings Cocoa Processing Company.

Rationale for selecting profiled firms. Cadbury, Cargill, Plot Enterprise and Archer Daniels Midland are among the largest cocoa processing facilities in Ghana. Real Products is an important new large-scale entrant to the industry.

2.2   Profiles of Major Firms

2.2.1   Real Products Limited

Basic details. Real Products is a recently established foreign-owned Free Zones company, set up to process about 50,000 mt of cocoa beans into finished and semi-finished products, largely for export. Real Products is located at Apowa in the Western region. The company has completed installation of plant and equipment and has carried out test runs. Production is due to start in March 2012.

The company already employs about 115 people and aims at an expected annual turnover of US$10 million.

History. In 1992, the Ecuadorian company Triairi SA Ecuador acquired Cafiesa (Ecuadorian Cacao Fino SA), a cocoa processing plant that had been in operation since 1974 in Guayaquil, Ecuador.

In 2007, Triairi SA established direct relationships with Ghanaian farmers and suppliers for the supply of quality cocoa beans for processing. Once these relationships were in place, Real Products was established in Ghana in 2010.

Current activities and products. Real Products processes cocoa beans into natural cocoa butter, natural cocoa liquor and natural and alkalized cocoa powder for export. As a Free Zones company, Real Products is committed to exporting a minimum of 70% of total production.

Organization and management. Real Products has a five-member board of directors. The management team includes the managing director and several functional heads.

Firm capabilities. Real Products has a complete cocoa processing capability with a capacity of 50,000 mt of cocoa beans annually. The production technology meets international food processing standards and will benefit from proprietary methods developed by the parent company. The production process includes laboratory analyses of the physical, chemical and organoleptic characteristics of beans before roasting and milling.

Competition. The firm's competitors include West African Mills Company Limited, Plot Enterprise Ghana and other processing facilities in the Greater Accra and Ashanti regions.

Supply and marketing chain. The main input (cocoa) will be acquired from the Western region, which is the leading cocoa producing region. The company will also source beans from Ivory Coast should the need arise.
Finished products will be supplied through the supply chain of the parent company: Triairi SA Equator.

Exports. Real Products will export a minimum of 70% of its production to its parent company and the remaining output will be sold on the local market.

Challenges. The company's main current concern is the high cost of power.

Development agenda. The company aims to expand its production from 50,000 mt to 150,000 mt within the next five years.

2.2.2   Plot Enterprise Ghana Limited

Basic details.   Plot Enterprise Ghana is registered in Ghana as a Free Zones company. The plant was completed in late 2009 as a turnkey project by Buhler Barth of Germany. This state-of-the-art grinding facility is located in Takoradi, gateway to the Western region, which is one of the highest cocoa producing areas in Ghana. It is located a few minutes' drive from the new 100,000 mt cocoa storage warehouse belonging to the CMC.

   The company has a total of 111 staff and an annual turnover of US$75 million.

History.   Plot Enterprise Ghana is wholly Ghanaian owned. Prior to the establishment of the plant, Patricia Poku-Diaby, the main founder of the company, was involved in the family business (trading and transportation). She later set up the Plot Enterprise Group in Ivory Coast, which was a precursor to the Ghanaian company. The group has market presence in Asia and West Africa and comprises Plot Commodities (registered with the Dubai Metal and Commodities Centre in Dubai), Plot Enterprise in Ivory Coast and Plot Enterprise Ghana. Plot Commodities deals in cotton and cocoa and is registered with the Cocoa Merchants Association of America. Plot Enterprise in Ivory Coast is engaged in the trading of cocoa, cashew nut and wood products.

   Plot Enterprise Ghana has an annual initial bean input capacity of 32,000 mt. The implementation of the project began in 2006 with trial runs starting in November 2009; the plant was fully commissioned in January 2010.

Current activities and products.   From its 32,000 mt input capacity, Plot has a total output of 25,600 mt of liquor, butter and cake.

Organization and management.   The management team is made up of the chief executive officer (CEO), who reports to an eight-member board, and the general manager, who oversees daily operation. The management team includes a plant manager, a finance and administration manager, a quality control manager, a production manager, a maintenance manager, a process engineer and a food safety team leader.

Firm capabilities.   Plot Enterprise Ghana is ISO 22000, kosher and Hazard Analysis & Critical Control Point certified. Plot is undertaking the process of obtaining accreditations – such as Rainforest Alliance, UTZ[6] and organic – for processing certified and traceable cocoa. Operational processes are

---

[6] UTZ means 'good inside' in the Mayan languages.

controlled automatically and operating standards are at European levels. The firm intends to expand from an input capacity of 32,000 mt to one of 48,000 mt.

Competition.   The main competitors in the Western region are WAMCO and Real Products. In the Ashanti region, the competitor is ADM. In the Greater Accra region, the main competitors are Cocoa Processing Company, Cargill, Barry Callebaut and Afrotropic.

Supply and marketing chain.   Cocoa beans are sourced from the CMC.

Exports.   Plot Enterprise Ghana exports to the US, Europe, Asia, Australia and the Middle East.

Challenges.   Ghana's Cocoa Board only exports beans of a certain minimum size. The slightly smaller beans remain in the country and are sold to processors located in Ghana. Having access to enough of these cheaper beans is vital for Plot.

Another concern is the volatility of the cocoa market. For example, the second half of 2011 saw the world price of cocoa beans drop by more than 40%.

Development agenda.   Plot Enterprise Ghana aims to extend its product range into deodorized butter.

2.2.3   Cadbury–Kraft Foods Ghana Limited

Basic details.   Cadbury–Kraft Ghana is a subsidiary of the multinational food and beverage manufacturer Kraft Foods Incorporated. The company has operated in Ghana for over 100 years and is located in Accra.

Cadbury–Kraft Ghana has a workforce of 250 employees and its annual turnover is US$18.75 million.

History.   The Cadbury company, which was established in the 1840s in the UK, set up a warehouse operation in Ghana in 1908 to source high-quality cocoa beans. The warehouse was converted to a manufacturing facility in 1948. In 1968 the firm was officially registered as Cadbury Ghana Limited. The original product lines (Bournita, Quench and chocolate spread) were later extended to include confectionery. In 2008 the confectionery plant in Ghana was closed and its operations transferred to Cadbury's facilities in Nigeria.

In 2010 Cadbury Ghana was taken over by Kraft Foods. Cadbury Ghana consequently became Cadbury–Kraft Foods Ghana Limited, a wholly owned subsidiary of Kraft Foods Incorporated.

Current activities and products. Cadbury–Kraft's current activities cover the production and export of cocoa and confectionery products. The company produces a drinking chocolate drink called Richoco in Ghana. Other Cadbury products (Hacks, Ahomka Ginger and Tom Tom) are produced at Cadbury's facility in Nigeria for distribution in Ghana.

Organization and management. Cadbury–Kraft has a four-member board and a management team comprising the managing director and heads of department for human resources, finance, sales, commercial, customer service, manufacturing and logistics.

Competition. The company's main competitor in the chocolate market is the Cocoa Processing Company. Nestlé Ghana Limited is its main competitor in chocolate drinks.

Supply and marketing chain. Milk powder and sugar are imported from Europe; cocoa powder is sourced locally. Products are distributed from a distribution centre in Tema, via distribution agents throughout the country. Cadbury also distributes directly to hotels, supermarket chains and petrol stations.

Exports. Cadbury–Kraft Ghana exports its chocolate drink, Richoco, to other African countries via its parent company.

Challenges. High import duties and the fluctuating price of cocoa as well as the high local cost of borrowing are leading concerns.

Development agenda. In the next five years Kraft Foods Incorporated aims to expand its business in emerging markets within Africa and Asia.

2.2.4   *Cargill Ghana Limited*

Basic details. Cargill Ghana, a subsidiary of the multinational group Cargill, is the country's largest exporter of processed cocoa products.

Cargill has a work force of 200 permanent staff and 200 contract/support staff.

History. Cargill began with William Wallace Cargill's first grain storage facility on the American frontier in 1865. A privately held company, it has four areas of business: agricultural services; food ingredients and applications; origination and processing; and risk management and financial.

In 2006 Cargill International opened its office in Ghana, which was then located in East Legon, a suburb of Accra. In 2007 the company set up its first cocoa processing facility in Tema, which became fully operational in 2008.

Current activities and products. The company supplies high-quality cocoa powders and cocoa butter to global food manufacturers of chocolate, biscuits, chocolate drinks and ice cream. The company processes 65,000 mt of cocoa beans annually to produce 45,000 mt of cocoa powder and 20,000 mt of cocoa butter.

Organization and management. Cargill Ghana has a four-member board of directors and a management team comprising the managing director, the finance director, the operations director and the human resources director. It has three expatriate staff on its management team.

Firm capabilities. The company operates a world-class facility supported by almost 50 years' experience as a cocoa processor. Through its global network, Cargill transfers expertise and personnel to Cargill Ghana as well as providing technical assistance.

Competition. Cargill Ghana's local competitors are Barry Callebaut, ADM Ghana and the Cocoa Processing Company Limited. The parent companies of Barry Callebaut and ADM Ghana compete with Cargill on the international market.

Supply and marketing chain. Cargill Ghana sources cocoa beans from the Ghana Cocoa Board. Carton boxes and wrappers are sourced locally. Chemicals and bags for packaging are imported from Europe. The company also imports spare parts and consumables for its cocoa processing plant.

Beans are transported by trucks to the factory, where they are roasted and processed. The powder and butter are wrapped and packaged into cartons that are transported to warehouses for shipment to the local market or to Cargill International.

Exports. Cargill exports all the cocoa butter it produces to Europe, where it is used for chocolates, coatings, etc. The company exports 50–70% of its cocoa powder to Europe and the US. The remaining 30–50% is sold locally to beverage producers in Ghana.

Challenges. The main issues facing the company are fluctuating commodity prices and the increasing cost of utilities.

Development agenda. The company aims to expand its operations and export activities to other countries.

2.2.5   ADM Cocoa (Ghana) Limited

Basic details. ADM Cocoa (Ghana) Limited, a subsidiary of the Archer Daniels Midland Group, produces cocoa liquor and ingredients for chocolate manufacturing. The company's offices and factory are located in Kumasi in the Ashanti region.

ADM Cocoa (Ghana) Limited has a workforce of 83 permanent staff, 13 temporary staff and 150 contract staff.

History. The Archer Daniels Midland Company was founded in the US in 1902 by George A. Archer and John W. Daniels, two entrepreneurs who began a linseed crushing business named Archer Daniels Linseed Company. In 1923, they purchased Midland Linseed Products Company, leading to the formation of Archer Daniels Midland.

Between 1923 and 1939 the company expanded into the crushing of soybeans, flour milling operations and the manufacture of formula feeds. By 1940 ADM had begun research into turning raw linseed and crude soybean oil into hundreds of different products.

From 1940 to 2000 ADM expanded its range of activities and its geographical reach. The company currently processes oilseeds, corn, wheat and cocoa for use in food products and animal feed and for industrial and energy uses. The ADM Group has 30,000 employees worldwide, with 265 processing plants, 400 crop procurement facilities and the world's premier crop transportation network. The group is present in more than 160 countries.

In 2005, ADM opened its first project office in Ghana with the aim of exploring cocoa processing opportunities. The company already had operations in the Ivory Coast and Cameroon. In 2007, ADM Cocoa (Ghana) Limited was incorporated and began construction of its cocoa processing facility/factory in Kumasi. The facility was completed in early 2009 and began production in July of the that year.

Current activities and products. ADM Cocoa (Ghana) Limited's primary activity is cocoa processing. The company processes cocoa beans into cocoa liquor, a semi-finished product.

Organization and management. ADM Cocoa (Ghana) Limited has a four-member board of directors. The company's management team is made up of a general manager, a plant manager and the heads of department of the finance, human resources, production/maintenance, logistics, IT/process control, quality control, and safety and environment divisions.

Firm capabilities. The company's capabilities lie in its state-of-the-art facilities for cocoa processing.

Competition. ADM Cocoa (Ghana) Limited's competitors are Cocoa Processing Company Limited, Cargill Ghana Limited and Barry Callebaut Ghana Limited.

Supply and marketing chain. The company sources its primary raw material, cocoa beans, from the Cocoa Marketing Company in Ghana (a subsidiary of the Ghana Cocoa Board). ADM Cocoa (Ghana) Limited sources all its packaging materials locally, while containers for storing the products for export are imported.

During processing, the beans are broken, roasted, ground and compressed to produce the cocoa liquor.

Exports. ADM Cocoa (Ghana) Limited exports all its final product, cocoa liquor, to Europe and the US.

Chapter 3

SALT PRODUCTION

3.1 Sector Profile

Background and overview. Ghana is a major salt producer, with annual production fluctuating between 250,000 mt and 350,000 mt.[1] Almost all production is of sea salt, which is produced in four regions: Greater Accra, Central, Volta and Western regions. Rock salt is produced in Daboya in the Northern region on an artisanal scale.

There are about 85 companies licensed by the Minerals Commission to produce salt. The total salt concession is 30,363 hectares.[2]

Structure of the industry. There are four categories of producer: large scale, medium scale, small and micro scale, and artisanal. The large-scale producers comprise firms and establishments with production capacities of between 30,000 mt and 100,000 mt per annum. Panbros Salt Industries Limited is the largest firm with production ranging between 60,000 mt and 70,000 mt, which represents 26% of national salt production. Ada Songor Salt Company, the second largest salt producer in Ghana, produces 40,000 mt of salt per year, or 16% of total production (Tables 3.1 and 3.2).

Five medium-scale companies produce between 5,000 mt and 29,000 mt per annum: Ningo Salt Limited, Edinaman Salt Limited, Dangbe Salt Industries, U2 Company Limited and Eldin Salt Limited.

The remaining firms are small- and micro-scale entities that produce between 50 mt and 1,500 mt per annum. The Presidential Special Initiative (PSI) on Salt estimates that there are 1,000 or so micro-scale salt producers, some of which are organized into cooperatives.

[1] Sync Consult Limited (for the International Finance Corporation). 2008. *Feasibility Study: Large-Scale Salt Production in Southern Ghana.*
[2] Source: Minerals Commission, Ghana (2008).

TABLE 3.1. Distribution of salt mining leases to
large and medium-size companies.

Region	Number of companies	Total salt concession (hectares)	Percentage of total concession
Greater Accra	27	18,782	61.90
Central	49	6,504	21.40
Volta	6	5,032	16.60
Western	3	46	0.10
Total	85	30,364	100

Some one million individual producers, referred to as salt winners, are organized into cooperatives that are found in Elimina, Anomabu, Nyanyano and Apam in the Central region and in Ada Songor in the Greater Accra region.[3]

Supply and marketing chain. About 20% of salt produced in Ghana is consumed locally. Small producers sell either to intermediaries or else to large buyers such as Unilever. The remaining 80% of production is exported to Burkina Faso, Mali, Niger, Togo and Benin.

Some companies, such as Ningo Salt Limited, U2 Salt Limited and Eldin Salt Limited, produce iodated salt under contract for Unilever.

Policy context. Since 2002 there have initiatives by government to

- develop links from the salt industry to the petrochemical industry,
- enhance land-use policies and operating technologies to harness the potential of the Keta and Songhor basins, which could produce an estimated one million metric tons annually, and
- establish land banks along the coast for sea salt production.

Over the past decade the government has focussed on addressing constraints facing the sector. The PSI on Salt was established to

- facilitate the identification and application of state-of-the-art technology,[4]
- facilitate the establishment or extension of 30 companies to produce 50,000–100,000 mt per annum based on the Corporate Village Enterprise model,

---

[3] Source: Presidential Special Initiative on Salt.
[4] These initiatives have not been developed due to a lack of funds.

TABLE 3.2. Annual and potential salt production capacity in Ghana.

No.	Company	Annual production (mt per annum)	Potential production (mt per annum)
1	Ada Songhor Salt Project	65,000	200,000
2	Panbros Salt Industries Limited	60,000	140,000
3	Eldin Salt	20,000	135,000
4	Ningo Salt Works	15,000	40,000
5	Tradevco	10,000	20,000
6	U2 Salt	5,000	30,000
7	Modern Salt	5,000	220,000
8	John Harris	1,500	42,000
9	Trans Volta	1,000	4,000
10	Caba	1,000	2,500
11	Pakat	1,000	2,000
12	Petua	1,000	13,000
13	Savannah	1,000	28,000
14	Adjua Salt	1,000	5,000
15	Nartey Salt	1,000	10,000
16	Ada Salt Producers Association (250 members)	50,000	150,000
17	Elmina Salt Producers Association (7 members)	5,000	8,000
18	Nyanyano Salt Producers Association (200 members)	2,500	30,000
19	Apam Salt Producers Association (16 members)	750	10,000
20	Keta Salt Winners Cooperation (85 members)	750	5,000
21	Anomabu Salt Producers Association (14 members)	500	2,000
22	Anlo-Afiadenyigba Salt Winners Cooperation (120 members)	300	7,500
23	Adina Salt Winners Cooperative (112 members)	100	2,000
24	Total	265,000	981,000

Source: Ministry of Trade and Industry (2009).

- facilitate the establishment of companies with annual capacities ranging between 250,000 mt and 450,000 mt, which are expected to serve as the main driving force for the development of the salt industry in Ghana (three projects have already been identified),
- develop unencumbered land banks suitable for salt production by the district assemblies in salt producing areas, and

TABLE 3.3. Export and import values of salt, 2005–2010.

Year	Export value (US$)	Import value (US$)
2005	49,379	227,016
2006	355,637	199,417
2007	788,397	140,253
2008	792,769	352,410
2009	651,563	665,481
2010	639,268	580,288

Source: Ghana Statistical Service (2010).

- find a lasting solution to the problems inhibiting industrial-scale salt production in the Ada Songor Basin (the biggest salt producing basin in Ghana).

Challenges. The production of sea salt using solar drying is highly seasonal. Production ceases during the rainy season, which lasts four to five months. (None of Ghana's facilities use vacuum technology.) This raises the overall cost of production.

The cost of transporting salt to markets in the West African subregion by road is sometimes twice the price of the commodity itself.

Poor infrastructure and a lack of financing for firms are also continuing concerns.

Competitiveness. Only processed salt is produced in Ghana and no company produces refined salt. This makes it difficult to compete internationally with producers from Brazil, Chile and Australia.

Export status, strength and potential. Ghana currently exports up to 80% of its salt to other Economic Community of West African States (ECOWAS) countries.

Ghana's proximity to West Africa and Europe offers a substantial opportunity if high-quality refined salt can be produced using modern technology and equipment. Current demand in West Africa (1.5 mt) is three times the supply of 550,000 mt currently produced by Ghana and Senegal, the shortfall being met from countries such as Brazil.

Four main categories of salt are exported from or imported into Ghana. These are salt for human consumption (including table salt), denatured salt, compressed salt and other salts. Export and import values of salt between 2005 and 2010 are presented in Table 3.3.

Recent developments. The commencement of commercial production of oil marks a potential turning point for the salt industry. Ghana is now in a position to develop a chlor-akali industry with linkages to the soaps and detergents, plastics, paints, pharmaceuticals, textiles, paper and metallurgical industries.

Rationale for selecting profiled firm. Panbros Salt Industries is the leading firm in the industry, accounting for 26% of production.

3.2   Profile of Major Firm

3.2.1   *Panbros Salt Industries Limited*

Basic details. Panbros Salt Industries is a limited liability company established in 1956. Located at Mendskrom in the west of the Greater Accra region, about 10 km from the city centre, it is the biggest salt works in Ghana, with a total area of 936 hectares and a production capacity of 75,000 mt per annum.

The company employs about 120 permanent staff and 200 casual staff. Additionally, the company has engaged contractors for the harvesting of salt that employ about 800 people in total. The turnover of the company was about US$3.3 million in 2010.

History. Panbros Salt Industries was founded by two Greek brothers, the Panagiotopolous brothers, who came into Ghana prior to independence and established two salt works there: Panbros Salt Industries in Accra and another smaller salt works in Elimina in the Central region of Ghana.

The Panagiotopolous brothers managed Panbros Salt Industries until 1970, when they sold their interest to a Ghanaian entrepreneur, Samuel Christian Appenteng, then a trader in several products. The company has remained a family business with private shareholders. The new owners of the company have continued to trade under the original name to this day.

Current activities and products. The company produces three main types of product: (i) coarse raw salt, which is harvested salt that has been iodated and bagged; (ii) washed salt, which is coarse raw salt that has been washed to remove shells, sand, etc.; and (iii) refined salt. Locally, 'refined' salt refers to raw coarse salt that has been thoroughly washed, ground into smaller granules and dried.

The company produces solar salt using a production method that depends entirely on the weather. It involves the channelling of sea water into solar ponds that are allowed to evaporate and eventually crystallize in the sun. Southern Ghana has an annual rainy season of four to five months during which the company is unable to produce salt. Consequently, it operates at 53% of its notional full capacity.

Organization and management.   The organization of the company comprises a board and a management team supported by functional heads in the areas of production, quality assurance, engineering, finance, administration and marketing. Although the company is a family business, the current managing director, Michael Odartey-Wellington, is not a member of the family.

Firm capabilities.   Being the oldest salt works in Ghana, Panbros Salt Industries has developed considerable expertise in solar salt production and harvesting. The company has become synonymous with salt production in Ghana.

Competition.   The main competitor of Panbros Salt Industries is the Ada Songor Salt Company. This is located in the Ada Songor area to the east of Accra, which has the largest salt basin in West Africa with a capacity to produce over 1.2 million mt of salt per annum. However, due to ownership problems with the land, the Ada Songor Salt Company has not realized its full potential and produces about 65,000 mt of salt annually. Other smaller competitors such as Ningo Salt Limited and Eldin Salt Limited have production volumes below 20,000 mt per annum. A large number of small salt producers in the Central region produce very small quantities.

Supply and marketing chain.   Potassium iodate, anticaking agent and pumps are imported from Germany, India and Austria.

Most output is sold at the factory to distributors, traders and wholesalers, who transport the product to the various markets in Ghana and to other countries in West Africa. The company also sells directly to clients.

Exports.   The company's raw salt is exported to Burkina Faso, Niger and Togo for use in leather tanning, textiles and animal feed. The salt is also processed in these countries for human consumption. Washed salt goes mainly to the local market, though some is exported to Ivory Coast.

Challenges.   The main issue facing the company is the trend that has been evident in recent years towards a longer rainy season, which has shortened the annual production period. Increased rainfall has caused flooding of the crystallization ponds and disruption of production. Other issues include environmental degradation as a result of sand winning on the beaches and pollution of the sea by waste from surrounding communities that dump waste into the Densu River (which flows into the sea close to the facility). Panbros Salt Industries is also concerned about encroachment on land reserved for its expansion.

Recent developments. The launch of the PSI on Salt in the last six years was expected to transform Ghana into a major producer of salt to serve the needs of most landlocked West African countries. However, the PSI is yet to make an impact; most of the planned programmes and interventions are yet to be implemented.

Development agenda. The company is aiming to acquire new plant and technology, and to increase its production capacity utilization from the current 53% to 87%. With this in mind, the company has been considering a vacuum salt production technology that would enable it to produce salt all year round and also to produce top-quality refined salt for use in the pharmaceutical sector.

Chapter 4

OIL PALM INDUSTRY

4.1 Sector Profile

Background and overview. The oil palm industry is an emerging sector in the Ghanaian economy with annual production averaging 100,000 mt.

Structure of the industry. The industry comprises three groups of firms: large, medium-size and small companies. There are four large companies – Ghana Oil Palm Development Company (GOPDC), Twifo Oil Palm Plantation (TOPP), Benso Oil Palm Plantation (BOPP) and Norwegian Palm Ghana Limited (NORPALM) – that have developed plantations on land compulsorily acquired by the government and that have plantations with processing capacities above 20 mt of fresh fruit bunches (FFBs) per hour. Together they account for 25% of the country's total production. Medium-size companies, with processing capacities between 2 mt and 20 mt of FFBs per hour, include Ayiem Oil Mills, Juaben Oil Mills, Adansi Oil Mills and Anyinase Oil Mills. These medium-size firms account for 15% of Ghana's total production. A large number of small producers, processing 0.5–2 mt of FFBs per hour, account for the remaining 60% of total production.

Oil palm fruits from the plantations are processed either into semi-processed products for sale to the industrial sector or into oil for household consumption. The domestic industrial sector accounts for over 70% of demand, using the oil as an input into the manufacture of soaps and margarine. Unilever Ghana Limited is the single largest consumer of palm oil in Ghana. PZ Cussons Limited, Appiah Menka Complex, Fats and Oils Limited and Ameen Sangari also use significant quantities. The degree of processing and refining varies widely. For example, crude palm oil sometimes undergoes further processing into refined bleached deodorized oil and palm fatty acid distillate. Refined bleached deodorized oil is then fractionated into palm olein and stearin. Further processing may remove fatty acids, odour or colour and produce a more free-flowing material, as well as hard fats used by bakeries.

Oil cake, which is separated out in the palm oil mill, is further separated into fibres and nuts. Most fibres are conveyed to the steam boiler as fuel and the nuts go to a nut breaker for cracking to obtain shells and kernels. The shells also go to the steam boiler as fuel. Palm kernels pass through drying silos and into a crushing plant to produce (crude or refined) palm kernel oil.

Supply and marketing chain.   Major industrial users such as Unilever are supplied directly by the producers. Small industrial users and retailers are supplied through intermediaries.

Policy context.   The sector is viewed by the government as having the potential to contribute significantly to the country's export earnings. As a result, the government has introduced various policy initiatives culminating in the establishment of the PSI on Oil Palm.

The Ghana Oil Palm Development Association formerly fixed prices, but its role has declined over the last decade. The PSI on Oil Palm aims to restructure the Ghana Oil Palm Development Association into an industrial cluster.

Challenges.   The high cost of electricity is seen as one of the most important issues facing the oil palm mills. In addition, the long gestation period of palm plantations and the substantial capital commitment required limit the growth of the industry, given the difficulties in accessing financing and the high level of local interest rates. Access to suitable land also poses problems.

Competitiveness.   The four large companies have significant advantages over their domestic rivals. Besides owning their own plantations, they support palm fruit production among peasants through nucleus estates and through smallholder and outgrower schemes to guarantee raw oil palm supply. The high throughput of the big companies enables them to generate sufficient waste fibre and kernel shell to fuel boilers to generate power. This both gives them cost savings and also reduces reliance on the national grid, which is prone to outages.

On the international market, low production volumes, shortcomings in technology and relatively high production costs make it difficult for Ghana to compete with countries such as Malaysia. Analysts are of the view that the country can make inroads into the international market when production levels are significantly increased and the level of technology improved.

Exports.   Some crude oil palm, palm kennel oil and palm kennel cake is exported to the US, South America and Europe.

Recent developments.   The government has, in the past decade, provided about US$3 million to establish some 32 nurseries. In addition, the government has commissioned the Oil Palm Research Institute (OPRI) to produce three million germinated oil palm seeds annually for the PSI on Oil Palm. Since 2004, 13,568 additional hectares of land have been brought under cultivation by participating groups under the PSI. In the medium to long term, 300,000 hectares is expected to be cultivated. The government is also seeking to turn about 68,000 hectares of degraded mining land over to cultivation of oil palm under the PSI. The PSI supports 60 milling factories to facilitate the establishment of vegetable oil refineries and biodiesel plants. In the long term, the oil palm sector is expected to generate US$1.6 billion in export revenue annually.

Profile of selected companies.

Ghana Oil Palm Development Company (GOPDC). The activities of the GOPDC include the organic cultivation of oil palm, the processing of FFBs in the mill to produce crude palm oil and palm kernel oil, and the refining/fractionation of crude palm oil into higher-value products. A full profile is given in Section 4.2.1 below.

GOPDC has two industrial plantations: the Kwae estate near Kade, in the Eastern region, and the Okumaning estate. The Kwae estate has a total concession of 8,953 hectares, of which approximately 5,205 hectares are developed, whereas the Okumaning estate has a total concession of 5,200 hectares, of which about 2,500 hectares have been developed. The company has a total of 2.9 million oil palm trees and has developed about 7,000 hectares of the total 21,000 hectares of oil palm plantations for outgrowers who own land located within 30 km of the oil palm mill. It also has an aggregate storage capacity of 16,000 mt both at Kwae and Tema and a modern refinery/fractionation plant with a capacity of 100 mt per day.

Twifo Oil Palm Plantation (TOPP) is an agricultural project initiated by the government of Ghana in 1977 with loan financing from the EU, the Commonwealth Development Corporation, the Netherlands Development Finance Company (Nederlandse Financierings–Maatschappij voor Ontwikkelingslanden NV; or FMO) and the government of the Netherlands. Work on the plantation commenced in August 1978. The core business of the company includes the running of plantations of oil palm and of other agricultural products, and the processing of oil palm fruits to produce palm oil and palm kernels. The company has a total of 4,234 hectares of oil palm in the Twifo–Hemang–Lower Denkyira district in the Central region.

The company has a processing capacity of 20 mt of FFBs an hour and annual production of about 17,000 mt of palm oil and 5,000 mt of palm kernel. The major shareholders of TOPP are the government of Ghana and Unilever Ghana Ltd. The estate is situated in the Twifo Ntafrewaso/ Twifo Mampong area. It has 2,450 hectares of mature oil palm, which were planted between 1979 and 1990.

Benso Oil Palm Plantation (BOPP) is a company that produces and processes crude palm oil. The company is located between Adum Banso and Benso in the Wassa Mpohor East district of the Western region.

The company also processes palm fruit from over 6,000 small farmers in the Western and Central regions.

BOPP is listed on the Ghana Stock Exchange and has an established record of strong profitability, reflecting very efficient management, and a highly skilled and dedicated workforce.

A full profile is given in Section 4.2.2 below.

Norwegian Palm Ghana Limited (NORPALM) is located at Prestea in the Ahanta West district of the Western region. NORPALM Ghana Ltd has a land concession of about 4,500 hectares at Prestea and 500 hectares at Sese. Some 70% of the company's input of FFBs is bought from outgrowers while the remaining 30% comes from its own estate.

The company manufactures crude palm oil, palm kennel oil and palm kennel cake, and it exports to North America, South America and Europe. It has estimated annual sales of US$100 million.

The company has a workforce of about 100 people (comprising both permanent and temporary staff).

Ayiem Oil Mills Limited (AOMIL), one of several medium-sized firms in the industry, is a Ghanaian private limited liability company located in Mpohor in the Western region. It has oil palm plantations in Ayiem, Abudukrom and Prestea. The company has a 237-hectare plantation in Ayiem, a 49-hectare plantation on the Abudukrom and a 68-hectare plantation in Prestea. The company has acquired another 971 hectares of land in Ayiem to expand its plantation.

The processing facilities of the company have two distinct sections; the palm oil processing section and the palm kernel oil processing section. The company has a capacity to process about 15,000 mt of palm oil annually.

Rationale for selecting profiled firms. Ghana Oil Palm Development Company is the largest producer of oil palm in Ghana. Benso Oil Palm Plantation is the second largest producer.

4.2 Profiles of Major Firms

4.2.1 Ghana Oil Palm Development Company

Basic details. GOPDC is a private limited liability company involved in oil palm planting, milling and refining. Located in the Kwaebibirem district in the Eastern region of Ghana, GOPDC owns two industrial plantations with a total concession of 14,153 hectares, of which 7,705 hectares have been developed. The company is jointly owned by SA Siat NV of Belgium, through Société d'Investissement pour l'Agriculture Tropicale (Siat-Ghana) Ltd (with a 70% ownership), and SSNIT and ATMF Ltd (Ghana) (30%).

GOPDC employs over 200 direct employees and over 10,000 indirect employees, including farmers and contract workers. The company has an average turnover of over US$40 million per annum.

History. GOPDC was established by the government of Ghana in 1975 to diversify agriculture through the cultivation of oil palm. The company operated as a state-owned facility until 1995, at which point it was privatized. Siat NV of Belgium, the majority shareholder, specializes in the development and management of industrial and smallholder plantations as well as allied processing and downstream industries.

The operations of GOPDC have been significantly expanded since privatization through the implementation of a growth plan and the infusion of new capital investment. The plan was developed for the period 2002–11. The aim was to add value to the products of the company as well as to increase the company's quality and efficiency.

Current activities and products. GOPDC currently produces nine main products:

 (i) crude palm oil (used for cooking and frying, in the production of dairy products, in nutritious supplements and in soap and detergent making);
 (ii) crude palm kernel oil (used for making ice cream, margarine, chocolate and confectionery products, soap and detergents);
 (iii) palm kernel cake;
 (iv) refined bleached deodorized oil;
 (v) refined palm kernel oil;
 (vi) palm fatty acid distillate;
 (vii) olein;
 (viii) super olein; and
 (ix) stearin.

Organization and management. GOPDC has a seven-member board of directors, and a four-member management team comprising the managing director, the deputy managing director, the chief financial officer and the chief agricultural officer.

Firm capabilities. The company's plant includes a 60 mt per hour FFB palm oil mill, a 60 mt per day kernel mill, a 100 mt per day refinery and fractionation plant, two tank farms, a 30 mt per hour boiler with a 2.5 megawatt turbine and a water treatment plant.

GOPDC was the first company to produce organic palm oil in Ghana and has been producing fully certified organic palm oil in conjunction with EcoCert International and Cirad-CP since 2002. The firm's capabilities include

- organic cultivation of oil palm, with over 2.9 million oil palm trees,
- the ability to extract crude palm oil and palm kernel oil, with a capacity to produce 35,000 mt per annum,
- the ability to store about 21,000 mt of products at its tank farms in Tema and Kwae, and
- the ability to produce refined specialty oils and fats used by the food industry.

Competition. The main competitors of GOPDC are NORPALM (the largest oil palm processing facility in Ghana), TOPP (a 4,234-hectare oil palm plantation and processing facility located in the Twifo–Hemang–Lower Denkyira district in the Central region), AOMIL (a Ghanaian private limited liability company located in Mpohor in the Western region of Ghana, with a capacity to process about 15,000 mt of palm oil annually) and BOPP (an oil palm plantation and processing facility located in Takoradi in the Western region).

Supply and marketing chain. All of the company's inputs are sourced locally with the exception of some varieties of seed nuts, which are purchased from Benin (Pobe) and Ivory Coast (Lame).

Finished products are supplied via distributors for the domestic market. Products are delivered in bulk from the company's tank farms. For export customers, products are pumped directly into vessels at the port of Tema.

Exports. The company exports to Nigeria, Senegal and Togo, as well as to Europe, the US, Asia and the Middle East.

Challenges. The main problems facing the company relate to pest beetles (which damage young plants), fungus and leaf miners (causing rapid defoliation of older palms). GOPDC is containing the beetles and fungus problems by employing good agricultural practice. The company is still working to find a permanent solution to the leaf miner problem.

A different area of concern is that during periods when prices fall on the international market some outgrowers that are supported by the company divert their products to the open market in violation of their contractual arrangement with GOPDC.

4.2.2 Benso Oil Palm Plantation

Basic details. BOPP cultivates oil palm from which FFBs are harvested and processed in its palm oil mill to produce crude palm oil. The palm kernel produced is processed (by a third party) to extract palm kernel oil.

The turnover of BOPP ranges between US$12.1 million and US$23.6 million per year.[1] The company has a staff strength of about 400 permanent employees and about 700 third-party (contract) employees.

History. BOPP was established in 1976 as a joint venture between UAC International (later Unilever Ghana) and the government of Ghana. The government held a 40% stake and UAC held 58.45%. In 2004 the government sold its shares on the stock exchange, and in March 2011 Unilever Ghana sold its shares to Wilmar Africa Limited, a subsidiary of Wilmar International, which is headquartered in Singapore. Wilmar Africa Limited currently holds a 76.5% share in the company.

Current activities and products. Wilmar uses BOPP as a secure source of crude palm oil. Production levels at BOPP are only half of Wilmar's crude palm oil requirements.

Demand for vegetable cooking oil in Ghana has increased while the output of crude palm oil has been static. Ghana is therefore currently a net importer of crude palm oil.

Palm kernel shells are bought by third parties who ship them to Europe for use as fuel.

Organization and management. Wilmar, as the majority shareholder, has overall control of the company via BOPP's board.

[1] Converted from Old Ghanaian Cedis (GH¢) at an average exchange rate of GH¢1.4 to US$1.00 (2010). The fluctuations in revenue reflect changes in world prices and climate conditions.

Competition. BOPP's competitors are NORPALM, AOMIL, TOPP and Ameen Sangari.

Supply and marketing chain. BOPP produces 70% of its main raw material, FFBs, and sources the remaining 30% from smallholders and outgrowers. Fertilizers and palm oil mill equipment are imported, mostly from Malaysia. The palm kernel oil and crude palm oil are sold at world market prices to Wilmar Africa Limited for production of cooking oil, margarine and soap.

Exports.   Even though Ghana is a net importer of crude palm oil, BOPP occasionally exports to West Africa, and in particular to Nigeria.

Recent developments. Environmental concerns raised against the oil palm industry in Indonesia are now affecting access to land for palm oil plantations in several regions.

Development agenda. The company aims to expand its operations through additional land acquisition with a view to closing the 50% gap between current industry production and demand from downstream manufacturing operations. Wilmar is also investing in capital assets to expand the capacity of its palm oil mill.

Chapter 5

AGRIBUSINESS AND FOOD PROCESSING

5.1   Sector Profile

Background and overview.   The agricultural sector plays a crucial role in the economy of Ghana. In addition to contributing 60% of formal and informal employment, the sector has contributed an average of 35% to GDP in the past five years.

The agricultural sector is segmented into crops (cereals and starchy crops such as cassava, plantain and yam), livestock, fisheries, forestry and cocoa.

Agribusiness in Ghana is still in the early stages of development and most agribusiness is artisanal, comprising activities such as gari processing and fish smoking. A large number of micro, small and medium-scale enterprises and establishments are involved in a wide range of business activities based on agriculture. Despite efforts by successive governments, there are no large-scale processing facilities that use the main agricultural produce of the country apart from those that process cocoa.

The supply chain of the agricultural sector involves farmers, stockists, middlemen, processors, marketers and consumers, as shown in Figure 5.1.

The growth of agribusiness is constrained by agricultural production capacity. Ghana is currently producing less than 30% of the raw materials needed by its agro-based industries.[1] The government acknowledges that the success of the agribusiness sector, especially agro-processing, will require sustained increases in agricultural productivity to guarantee continuous availability of raw materials. Consequently, the modernization of the agricultural sector is one of the main priorities of the government.

Information from the Ministry of Agriculture indicates that post-harvest losses are very high in Ghana and lie between 30% and 40%. The figure is higher for perishable products such as tomatoes, where losses in excess of 50% have been reported in the Ashanti, Brong Ahafo and Upper East regions. Factors contributing to the high incidence of post-harvest losses

---

[1] Business for Development–Ghana. 2008. *Agriculture Is Becoming a Business*. Organisation for Economic Co-operation and Development.

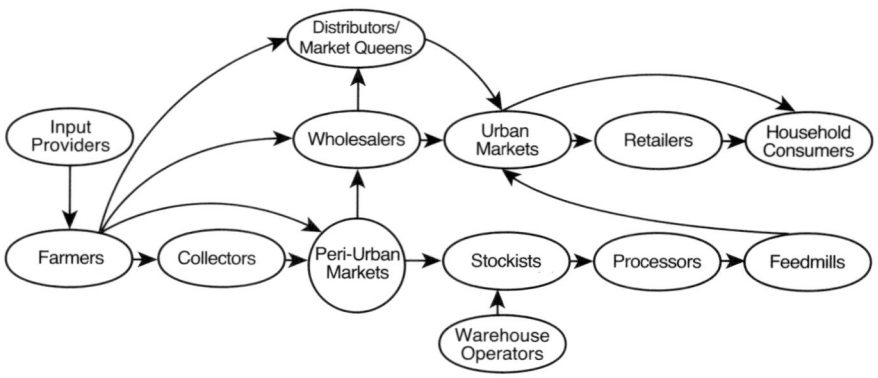

FIGURE 5.1. Typical agribusiness market chain.

in Ghana include an absence of well-developed preservation systems, poor infrastructure at the producing centres, lack of storage facilities, poor market access, lack of agro-processing facilities and poor marketing systems. The post-harvest problem is exacerbated by the highly perishable nature of most of the produce. Thus, high levels of production do not necessarily translate into the availability of food and food shortages can occur even when harvests are good.

Food processing. Food processing covers a range of activities including processing and preservation of meat, fish, fruit, vegetables, oils and fats; manufacture of dairy products; manufacture of grain mill products, starches and starch products and prepared animal feeds; and manufacture of other food products (e.g. bread, sugar, chocolate, pasta, coffee, nuts and spices).

The food processing business in Ghana is directly linked to the main agricultural produce of the country: maize, rice, plantain, cassava and yam. These can be processed into maize oil, maize flour, rice flour, fragrance rice, ground rice, dried cassava, cassava starch, cassava flour, cassava tapioca and finished food products such as pasta, noodles and maize powder meals (Figure 5.1).

The food processing industry in Ghana is relatively small and most of the activities in the sector are undertaken on a small scale. The main crops that are processed on a medium-to-large scale are maize and cassava. Maize is mainly processed into flour, while cassava is processed into flour, dried cassava, cassava dough and starch. Other products that are produced on a medium-to-large scale include flour (made from cassava,

TABLE 5.1. The trend in the production of major food crops in Ghana 2004–2010.

Crop	2004	2005	2006	2007	2008	2009	2010
Maize	1,157,600	1,171,400	1,189,000	1,219,600	1,470,100	1,619,600	1,619,590
Rice paddy	241,800	236,500	250,000	185,300	301,900	391,400	391,440
Millet	143,800	154,600	165,000	113,000	193,800	246,000	245,550
Sorghum	287,400	299,000	315,000	154,800	331,000	350,600	350,550
Cassava	9,738,200	9,567,200	9,638,000	10,217,900	11,351,100	12,230,600	12,230,630
Cocoyam	1,715,900	1,685,800	1,660,000	1,690,100	1,688,300	1,504,000	1,503,960
Yam	3,892,300	3,922,800	4,288,000	4,376,000	4,895,000	5,778,000	5,777,850
Plantain	2,380,800	2,791,600	2,900,000	3,234,000	3,338,000	3,563,000	3,562,500
Groundnuts	389,600	420,000	520,000	301,800	470,100	485,100	485,080
Total (mt)	19,947,400	20,248,900	20,675,000	21,492,500	24,039,300	26,168,300	26,167,150

Source: Statistics, Research and Information Directorate, Ministry of Food and Agriculture (December 2011).

rice and maize), dried cassava and gari, and value-added products such as Cerelac and Cerevita (a maize-based food cereal produced by Nestlé). Other major processing companies include ELSA Foods, Gracem Foods, Mannas Tropical Export and Kwanoye Ghana Co. Ltd.

Some processing activities, notably wheat flour milling, depend on imported inputs.

Flour processing. Flour is processed from a number of crops: wheat, cassava, yam, cocoyam, plantain, sorghum, maize and corn.

Corn flour is largely produced through local mills using locally grown corn. Corn is the main staple in Ghana and corn flour is made into local dishes (e.g. *banku, kenkey* and *akple*). Ghana produced about 1.62 million mt of maize in 2010: a 10% increase over the 1.47 million mt produced in 2009. Some maize is imported, mainly for the production of animal feed and fishmeal.

Other grains. Ghana also produces millet and sorghum. Beans are grown in large quantities as well. The main commercial activities involve processing into animal feed and fishmeal.

Wheat flour production depends totally on imported hard wheat from North America (for bread production) and soft wheat from Europe (for the pastries sector). Ghana imports between 100,000 mt and 150,000 mt of wheat annually, with supplies being split 80% from North America and 20% from the EU. The total volume of wheat flour production in Ghana was estimated at 171,832 mt in 2007, increasing to 211,887 mt in 2008.[2] Production grew over the past decade at an average annual growth rate of 13%. There are three flour mills in Ghana with a total installed capacity of 275,000 mt: Irani Brothers, Takoradi Flour Mill and Ghana China Food Company Limited.[3] A fourth mill, with a capacity of 50,000 mt, is currently under construction.

Ghana imports about 100,000 mt of wheat flour annually.[4] Some 95% of imported flour is soft wheat flour, which is used mainly for pastries and biscuits. Imported flour accounts for about 30% of demand.

Wheat flour is a major input for producers of bread, biscuits, macaroni and spaghetti.

---

[2] Ghana Statistical Service.

[3] One other wheat flour miller, Ghana Agriculture Food Company Limited, closed down in 2010.

[4] Ghana Statistical Service.

TABLE 5.2. Foreign exchange earnings from seafood exports.

Year	Value (millions of US$)
2000	18.58
2001	23.85
2002	24.48
2003	26.85
2004	52.02
2005	45.76
2006	67.90
2007	86.53
2008	61.00
2009	48.12

Source: Ghana Export Promotion Council (2010).

Wheat-based products.

Bread. Many small local bakeries operate across the country; a few medium-sized bakeries are found in supermarkets and large department stores.

Biscuits are manufactured by three companies: Parlays, Fairbon and Piccadilly Biscuits.

Fish processing.
Ghana's domestic fisheries production is estimated at 440,000 mt per annum. The sector contributes 4.5% to GDP and indirectly supports the livelihoods of 2.2 million people (10% of the population); see Table 5.2.

Ghana's artisanal fishing sector includes 10,000 small mechanized wooden boats that harvest 60–70% of the marine catch. About 170 larger semi-industrial ships with inboard motors are used for trawling in shallow waters during the off season and purse seining[5] during upwelling seasons. Approximately 90 industrial vessels are used for shrimping, tuna lines and poles, purse seining and demersal pair trawling.[6]

In the industrial sector, tuna production has increased significantly in recent years. The Food and Agriculture Organization estimates that the sustainable catch of tuna is 90,000–100,000 mt per year. Only 36,000 mt of tuna is currently landed.

---

[5] A purse seine is a net that is made up of a long wall of netting framed with a lead line of equal or longer length than the float line. It is usually used to fish tuna. Purse seining involves surrounding tuna schools with a net.

[6] Dem ersal pair trawling involves bottom trawling by two vessels that are towing the same net.

TABLE 5.3. Destination of Ghana's seafood exports (2009).

Market	Product
UK	Canned tuna
France	Canned tuna
Spain	Frozen tuna, other fish, cuttle fish
Italy	Lobster
Greece	Shrimps
Belgium	Prawns
US	Salted fish, crab
Togo	Smoked/dried fish
Hong Kong	Shark fin

Source: Ghana Investment Promotion Council (2010).

TABLE 5.4. The trend in the production of meat in Ghana, 2004–2010.

	2004	2005	2006	2007	2008	2009	2010
Cattle	18,686	18,874	19,140	19,347	19,553	19,768	19,990
Sheep	14,004	14,450	14,913	15,390	15,881	16,389	16,914
Goats	15,308	15,300	15,588	16,364	17,180	18,038	18,935
Pigs	9,979	9,744	16,027	16,498	17,002	17,512	18,026
Poultry	22,982	22,709	27,224	29,630	31,853	34,656	38,202
Total (mt)	80,959	81,077	92,892	97,229	101,469	106,363	112,067

Source: Statistics, Research and Information Directorate, Ministry of Food and Agriculture (December 2011).

Most of the catch is processed: 60% is smoked, 20% is salted and the remaining 20% is sold fresh. Most of the processing is undertaken in the informal sector, with smoking being the most widely used process.

The markets for Ghana's processed seafood are Europe, North America and Asia: the leading countries are shown in Table 5.3.

There are currently four major companies involved in fish processing in Ghana. Industrial fish processing largely covers tuna canning and tuna fishmeal production.

Meat processing. Commercial livestock production contributes about 7–10% of agricultural GDP. Total meat production increased from 80,959 mt in 2004 to 112,067 mt in 2010 (Table 5.4).

There are a large number of small and medium-scale poultry farms and piggeries, but no large-scale commercial farms.

Commercial production of farm animals has grown in response to increasing domestic meat consumption. The livestock population (poultry, sheep, goats, cattle and pigs) has increased at an annual average rate of 6% since the 1990s.

The total livestock population rose from 28 million in 2000 to 50 million in 2010. Poultry accounts for 76% of the total livestock population, goats 11%, sheep about 9% and cattle and pigs for about 5% between them.

Total meat production has been growing at an average annual rate of about 6% over the past five years: from 81,077 mt in 2005, total meat production increased to about 110,000 mt in 2010. It currently accounts for 30% of domestic consumption.

There is a huge cross-border trade in cattle and sheep from the Sahelian countries in West Africa (Mali, Niger, Burkina Faso, etc.) and this feeds into the domestic fresh meat market trade as the animals are transported live and slaughtered in Ghana. Ghana imports chicken from the Netherlands, pork products from Sweden, Denmark and the Netherlands, beef from France and Ireland, and turkey from the US.

Large-scale, commercial meat processing facilities are lacking and the country does not have a meat canning facility. Meat processing activities in Ghana are restricted to the small-scale production of sausages and bacon. Large quantities of sausages and bacon are imported as demand continues to grow. All canned meat products, such as corned beef, are imported from Argentina, the Netherlands and elsewhere.

Small and medium-sized enterprises (SMEs) such as Sotrec and Cottage Farms are the leading meat processors, focussing on sausage and bacon production.

Fruits and vegetables. Fruits and vegetables play a leading role in the industry. Pineapples are the major exported fruit while tomato is the major vegetable export. In view of its contribution to the foreign exchange earnings for the country (7.0% of GDP in 2009), the pineapple subsector has been the focus of several policy initiatives by the government of Ghana.

Ghana's pineapple exports increased from 18,777 mt in 2000 to 29,265 mt in 2010 (Figure 5.2).

Other fruits cultivated on a large scale are oranges, lemons, limes, grapes, ginger, mangoes, bananas, avocados and guavas.

Facilities for preservation, and wholesaling, are poor, and some 40% of fruit consumed in Ghana is imported from neighbouring countries.

Oils and fats. Oils and fats were originally processed by traditional methods. Over the past two decades, groundnut oil, palm nut oil and coconut oil have come to be produced on a larger scale. There are a few medium- and large-scale enterprises involved in oil production, as well as many

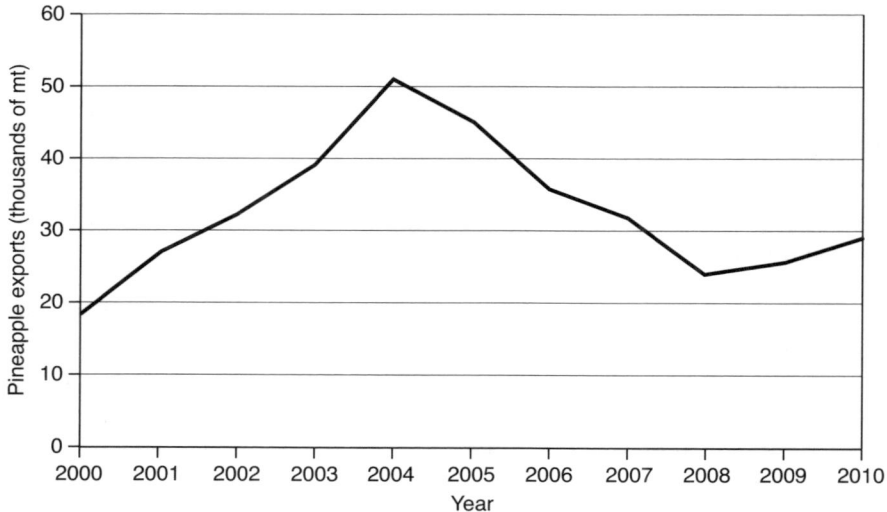

FIGURE 5.2. Pineapple exports, 2000–2010.
(Source: Sea-Freight Pineapple Exporters of Ghana (2011).)

small operations. Palm nut oil extraction is of particular importance due to export opportunities.

Ghana exports coconut oil but imports sunflower oil and olive oil.

Dairy products. Despite government attempts to establish cattle rearing and dairy facilities, Fan Milk Limited is currently the only major dairy products facility in Ghana. Fan Milk relies heavily on imports of milk products to meet its production requirements.

Sugar processing. The production of sugar in Ghana dates back to the 1960s, when the government set up two sugar factories at Komenda in the Western region and Asutuare in the Eastern region in 1966 and 1967. The plants, which marked the beginning of the sugar industry in Ghana, had a production capacity of about 45,000 mt. The Asutuare factory had an annual production capacity of 30,000 mt of sugar, while the sugar plant at Komenda had an annual production capacity of 15,000 mt. The factories encountered various operational difficulties and were closed down in 1983.

Ghana imports about 200,000 mt of sugar annually, valued at about US$100 million, from Brazil, France, Niger, Germany and South Africa. Brazil alone accounted for almost 50% of total imports.

The government, through the Ministry of Trade and Industry and the Ghana Investment Promotion Centre, seeks to support the establishment of sugar factories in Ghana. As a member of the International Sugar Organization,[7] Ghana offers favourable conditions for large-scale sugarcane cultivation in areas in the Central region, in the Western region and in parts of the northern savannah agro-ecological zones of the country.

Small-scale, informal and peripheral activities.

Small-scale butchers. There are several small-scale abattoirs that serve the needs of households, restaurants and local food vendors. As these abattoirs lacked appropriate facilities, the government established two large abattoirs in Accra and Kumasi in 1996.

Local mills. There are many small domestic mills, especially for corn, which sell directly to households.

Supply and marketing chain.   Supply chains for agribusinesses that rely on local agricultural produce such as maize, cassava and fruits are characterized by poor transportation infrastructure, poor storage systems and an absence of quality-assurance systems. The result is irregular deliveries, unreliable performance on supply contracts and a high cost of inputs.

For the wheat flour industry, import sources are reliable but importers depend on the mills to provide financing. Depreciation of the local currency against the US dollar can undermine the financial performance of the mills. In 2008, world wheat prices increased by over 200% and some Ghanaian mills almost went bankrupt.

The local distribution of flour to bakeries, biscuit manufacturers and other users is fairly smooth. The mills, through a network of regional depots and large distributors, cover the entire country with their product. Shortages of flour on the local market are rare occurrences, though price hikes can result from increases in world wheat prices.

Policy context.   As part of the strategy to promote expansion and growth in the agribusiness and food processing sector, the government has provided import duty exemptions for the importation of plant, machinery and equipment. In addition, companies engaged in agro-processing are entitled to a five-year tax holiday. Organizations such as the US Agency of International Development (USAID) are working with experts such as Technoserve and AMEX International and other foreign non-governmental

[7] The International Sugar Organization, which is based in London, is a unique intergovernmental body devoted to improving conditions on the world's sugar market through debate, analysis, special studies, transparent statistics, seminars, conferences and workshops. Its 84 member states represent 82% of world sugar production, 66% of world sugar consumption, 93% of world sugar exports and 38% of world sugar imports.

organizations to provide support to farmers in the areas of training, mentoring and the provision of technical support and equipment to help boost the productivity levels of this sector.[8]

Productivity is expected to be boosted by a number of technologies developed by Ghana's research institutes, including

- improved varieties of cassava, maize and rice, which have boosted yield, production volumes and exports (Crop Research Institute) and
- new technologies such as slicing, drying and fermentation equipment (Food Research Institute and Institute of Industrial Research).

Challenges.   Ghana's agricultural production currently supplies only half of domestic cereal and meat consumption and 60% of domestic fish consumption. Self-sufficiency is achieved only in starchy staples such as cassava, yam and plantain, while rice and maize production falls far below consumption.[9]

Agriculture is largely rain-fed, with traditional systems prevailing in most parts of the country. Poor irrigation infrastructure, infrequent adoption of the latest technology and small production volumes are continuing problems. Maize and rice are produced at a third of their potential yields per hectare.[10] Low public investment and the difficulties that SMEs encounter when trying to access finance limit the potential of agribusiness activities. Exports are limited by lack of capacity and the challenge of meeting EU and US food safety standards. The general inadequacy of supporting infrastructure, such as cold-chain facilities from the farm gate to the ports, the high costs of storage and the level of utility costs are among the key challenges facing the sector.

Competitiveness.   With the exception of freshly cut pineapples, which have made inroads into the EU market, most other areas of agribusiness cannot yet satisfy domestic demand.

Export status, strength and potential.   Ghana's proximity to Europe, and initiatives such as the African Growth and Opportunity Act (AGOA), offer significant opportunities. The Ministry of Trade and Industry has embarked on initiatives and programmes to promote Ghanaian products on the

---

[8] Ghana Investment Profile. 2011. *Food Production and Processing.* Ghana Investment Promotion Council.

[9] Business for Development–Ghana. 2008. *Agriculture is Becoming a Business.* Organisation for Economic Co-operation and Development.

[10] Business for Development–Ghana. 2008. *Agriculture is Becoming a Business.* Organisation for Economic Co-operation and Development.

world market. Trade shows have been organized in conjunction with other countries to promote Ghanaian agribusiness enterprises abroad.

Recent developments. The government has set up several facilities to provide credit to enterprises within the agribusiness sector. Among these, the government has partnered with several development agencies to support projects in the sector. The government, through the Agro-Processing Programme of the Ministry of Local Government and Rural Development, has entered into a partnership with Cottage Italia, an international partner, to offer credit for the importation of agro-processing equipment from Italy by Ghanaian SMEs.

Profiles and lines of business of large firms.   The following five firms are profiled in the next section.

Irani Brothers & Others Limited was established in 1967 to produce wheat flour for the bread and pastry industry. It accounts for about 60% of wheat flour sales in the country.

Takoradi Flour Mills Limited was established in the 1970s and produces both bread flour and pastry flour. It accounts for about 30% of wheat flour sales.

Unilever Ghana Limited is a subsidiary of Unilever PLC. Unilever Ghana not only produces food products but is active in production of home care and personal care products.

MW Brands (formerly Pioneer Food Cannery Limited) processes canned and cured fish and other seafood. The company, which trades under the name Starkist, is the major purchaser of tuna in Ghana. It is also the major purchaser of canned tuna and tuna loins as raw materials for other Starkist units.

Parlays Ghana Limited is one of Ghana's two leading biscuit makers (the other being Piccadilly Biscuits).

Profiles of selected medium-sized firms.

Sotrec Cold Store and Butchery Company is a wholly owned Ghanaian company established in 1987, Sotrec employs over 70 workers and has a turnover of US$1.3 million per annum.

Sotrec was established by Komla A. Hukportie, a Ghanaian who worked as a civil servant in Togo. A statistician and economist by profession, Hukportie returned to Ghana and set up Sotrec to trade in commodities. The company began by trading commodities such as cooking oil, rice, sugar and tomato paste. As the business grew, Hukportie began to import fish, and in 1989 he rented a cold store from the State Fishing Corporation in Tema for the fish business. He also subsequently extended his activities to the importation of meat.

While selling imported meat, Hukportie's attention was drawn to the unhygienic conditions of most abattoirs in Ghana and the poor meat processing procedures used by local butchers in the country. In 1988, Sotrec began processing meat on a small scale, employing professional butchers from Togo and the Netherlands to help set up the factory. In 1994 the company began to produce sausages, ham and bacon. In 1994 the company began sourcing meat from neighbouring herdsmen and local butchers from the Sahelian regions, such as Mali and Burkina Faso. Its first butcher shop was opened in a suburb of Accra in 1996.

The company's current products are sausages, ham, bacon, burgers and fresh meat cuts. Fresh meat carcasses from local butchers are deboned and cut into parts. Some spices and preservatives are imported, while ginger, garlic and pepper are sourced locally.

Some output is sold through the firm's own butcher shops and some is packaged and labelled for distribution to wholesale customers. The company supplies major hotels as well as large supermarket chains in Accra, Kumasi and Tema.

Nkulenu Industries Limited, established in 1942 by the late Dr Esther Ocloo, produces palm soup base (also known as banga soup), palm nut cream/concentrate, palm drink (palm wine or palm juice), canned garden eggs and aubergines, orange marmalade, pineapple jam and orange squash.

The company currently employs 50 workers in Madina, a suburb of Accra. Its turnover ranges between US$250,000 and US$500,000 per annum.

The business began when, on graduating from college, Ocloo began to make and sell orange marmalade and orange squash. She subsequently spent some time in the UK, studying food science and modern food processing techniques. On returning to Ghana, she extended her range of products. The company's present factory was constructed in 1962.

As the business expanded, Ocloo invested in new product development in the canning of fruit and vegetables.

One of the first canned products which Ocloo introduced was jollof rice,[11] which was sold to the Ghanaian army, then on a mission to the Democratic Republic of Congo. With food preservation its core business by 1970, the

[11] A popular Ghanaian dish made from rice and tomato sauce.

company introduced its first palm soup base (for preparing palm soup and stews) onto the Ghanaian market – bringing it the export market in 1972. This was followed by products such as canned palm nut cream, canned garden eggs and aubergines and palm drink, which are exported to Europe and the US, while orange squash, orange marmalade and pineapple jam are produced for the local market. Nkulenu has wholesalers and retailers in Ghana, Nigeria, the UK and the US.

Vision 2000 Farms is a commercial fish farm with headquarters 25 km from Accra. The company has an aquaculture farm located at Domeabra on the Volta Lake in the Volta region. The company employs 130 people and has an average turnover of US$1 million.

Vision 2000 Farms was established in 1999 by Samuel Ahiadeke, who previously owned and operated a block-making factory and traded in imported louver blades.

The farm produces fingerlings and matured tilapia. Vision 2000 farms has over 42 cages for its cage culture fisheries and produces between 2,500 mt and 3,000 mt of fresh tilapia per week. Additionally, the farm produces over 300,000 healthy fingerlings per week.

The farm imports fishmeal from Saudi Arabia and Brazil which it processes to feed its stocks. Inputs such as nets, ropes, plastic drums and wood used for building the cages are acquired locally. The farm also uses large volumes of locally sourced salt during the production of the fingerlings.

Gari processing. Gari is a dry coarse flour made from cassava. It is consumed as a staple in Nigeria, Ghana, Benin and Togo and in Central Africa.

Cassava is the second most important local food staple in Ghana after maize. It is grown in all regions with the exception of the Upper East and Upper West regions. Cassava production in Ghana ranges between 8.0 million mt and 10.2 million mt annually. The Brong Ahafo region, the leading producer of cassava in Ghana, has the highest yield of 14.5 mt per hectare. The Eastern region is the second biggest producer of cassava, with total annual production of about 2.1 million mt.

The Ghana Standards Authority (GSA)[12] defines gari as a 'dry pregelled particulate product obtained by artisanal or industrial processing of cassava roots'. The GSA specification defines the processing to consist of peeling, washing, grating, fermenting, de-watering, fragmenting, sifting and roasting to dryness by stirring. The GSA standards require gari to be free of any foreign matter. It also grades gari as extra fine, fine, medium size,

---

[12] The GSA used to be called the Ghana Standards Board.

coarse or unclassified. Most small processors are organized into groups. For example, in the Nkwanta district of the Volta region there are over 50 gari processing groups, with membership ranging between 10 and 15 processors.[13] The Progressive Women Movement in the Volta region has established a modern gari processing and training centre to serve the major producing communities in the Kpando district. The enterprise works with women's groups, each with an average membership of 30. The processed gari is sold to middlemen or is directly marketed and sold on the local market by small-scale producers. The Northern Volta Cassava Processors Association supports members to improve the production process and the quality of products such as cassava chips, flour and animal feed.

A number of SMEs export gari. These third-party exporters receive supplies from processors to fill orders from Europe and the US. Major exporters such as Elsa Foods, Obeng Foods and Domino Ventures export to order for their foreign clients.

The export of gari has been increasing steadily over the past five years. The total value of gari exports is about US$5 million.[14] There is a high demand for gari from immigrant African communities in the US, the UK and other European countries.

Rationale for selecting profiled firms. Irani Brothers is the largest flour mill in Ghana, with over 55% of the market share, and Takoradi Flour Mill is the second biggest, with 40% of the market share. Unilever is Ghana's largest and fastest-moving manufacturer of consumer goods. MV Brands is the largest fish cannery in Ghana. Parlays is the second largest biscuit factory in Ghana.

5.2   Profiles of Major Firms

5.2.1   *Irani Brothers & Others Limited*

Basic details. Irani Brothers & Others was established in 1967 to produce wheat flour for the bread industry. It is the oldest and largest wheat flour mill in the country. The company has its head office in Osu, Accra and its milling plant is in the Tema Industrial Area.

Irani Brothers employs 350 people and has an annual turnover of about $115 million (2010).

---

[13] Ministry of Food and Agriculture Ghana. 1997. *Cassava Development in Ghana: A Country Case Study of Cassava Development in Ghana.*
[14] Ghana Export Promotion Council.

History. The company was started by two Lebanese brothers, Anthony and Edmund Irani, who immigrated to Ghana. They provided the required start-up capital and have operated and managed the firm as a family business ever since.

Anthony and Edmund Irani, who both had technical expertise in the flour milling business, provided leadership for the company. One of the unique attributes of the company is that the two brothers developed and implemented a good succession plan to identify and develop the capacity of individuals within the Irani family to take up leadership positions in the company. This plan has contributed to the operational success of the company over the past 40 years. Although Anthony and Edmund Irani are both deceased, the managing director of the company is a member of the Irani family (a son-in-law of the founders). Irani Brothers & Others is one of the most successful of Ghana's second- and third-generation companies.

Current activities and products. Irani Brothers & Others currently produces two main products: bread flour and pastry flour. The extension to pastry flour was a response to the growth in domestic demand for the product that came with an expansion in the number and capacity of Ghana's biscuit factories and the entry of a large number of domestic pastry producers.

The company currently imports about 180,000 mt of wheat annually for milling into bread and pastry flour. The wheat flour is imported from Canada and the US.

Irani Brothers does not have sales and distribution outlets. It sells its products to wholesalers, retailers and end users directly from the factory.

Organization and management. The managing director, who reports directly to a three-member board of directors, is supported by a senior management team that manages daily operations and ensures compliance with legal, regulatory and company policy, controls and standards.

Firm capabilities. The core strength of Irani Brothers lies in its ability to source full shiploads of wheat and to secure the necessary funding arrangements; this gives it a competitive advantage over all the other flour mills in Ghana. No other flour mill has the capacity to continuously source wheat in large quantities. Irani Brothers has the largest flour milling capacity in Ghana and accounts for more than 50% of total wheat flour sales.

The company has three milling plants, all imported from Switzerland. The equipment is top of the range for the international wheat flour industry. The total installed capacity is about 150,000 mt per annum.

Competition.   The flour milling industry in Ghana was long dominated by four companies: Irani Brothers & Others, Takoradi Flour Mills, Ghana Agriculture Food Company Limited and Ghana China Food Company Limited (which produces under the brand name Tema Flour). Ghana Agriculture Food Company closed down some three years ago as a result of operational issues. As a result, there are currently only three companies serving the entire country. A fourth mill is currently under construction.

The total installed capacity of Ghana's mills falls short of total market demand. Irani Brothers is the market leader with about 55% of the total market, with installed capacity of 150,000 mt per annum. Takoradi Flour Mill, with 100,000 mt of installed capacity, accounts for about 40% of the market. Ghana China Food Company Limited, with an installed capacity of 50,000 mt, accounts for the remaining 5% of the market. The competitive environment is expected to change when Olam (a Singapore-based agricultural products supply chain management and food products company) completes construction of a 500 mt per day (115,000 mt per annum) flour mill in 2012.

In the pastry flour sector, there is some competition from imported pastry flour. However, imported flour sometimes deteriorates and the biscuit and pastry manufacturers prefer locally produced flour. Irani Brothers is the market leader in this segment.

Supply and marketing chain.   The process flow of the company starts with the arrival of wheat at the port, which is then transported to the silos. This is subsequently washed and sifted for milling. After the milling process, additives are introduced to the mixture, which is then bagged and sold.

The main issues facing Irani Brothers are the high cost of electricity and increases in the world market price of wheat.

Exports.   The company does not itself export. However, some of its customers export its flour to neighbouring countries. The company assists such distributors with the necessary labelling and other support.

Development agenda.   The company will continue to work closely with customers to provide support in training and to enhance productivity.

5.2.2   Takoradi Flour Mills Limited

Basic details.   Takoradi Flour Mills is a limited liability company located in Takoradi in the Western region of Ghana, about 220 km from Accra. It has 350 employees.

History. Takoradi Flour Mills was set up by an Armenian, Vasken Bakalian. It had an initial capacity of 200 mt per day and employed 60 people.

Currently, Takoradi Flour Mills has three plants with a total installed capacity of 1,000 mt per day. Two of the plants were manufactured in the UK and the other came from Switzerland. The workers who assisted with the installation were trained during the installation process. The installation experts stayed for an additional three months to train the local team and develop its capacity.

The company has three depots in Accra, Takoradi and Kumasi.

Since the death of Vasken Bakalian 20 years ago, a general manager, Thierry Loupiac, has provided leadership.

Takoradi Flour Mills has faced several issues in the past three decades. These difficulties included the downturn in the economy in the 1980s, which affected sales and financial performance. Its lack of financial resources made it difficult for the company to import wheat. Some workers were laid off temporarily. The energy crises of 1998 affected operations and Takoradi Flour Mills was unable to meet its targets. The Electricity Company of Ghana supported the company to ensure that it had electricity to remain in operation. The legal and regulatory environment within which the company operates is challenging, but the company strives to satisfy regulatory requirements laid down by the Environmental Protection Agency, the Ghana Fire Service and the Ghana Standards Board.

Current activities and products. The main products of Takoradi Flour Mills are bread flour and pastry flour. A residue is sold as wheat bran. The flour produced by the company is packaged and sold to end users under the Sunrise (Stool) brand name. Presently, the company processes about 3,500 mt of wheat weekly.

Besides the production of flour and bran, Takoradi Flour Mills provides training and capacity development advice to bakers. The training programmes are designed to inform bakers about how to get optimal results.

Organization and management. The organizational structure of the company comprises a board, a general manager, senior management, line managers and technical and support staff.

Firm capabilities. The company has an efficient and effective quality-assurance system that ensures that products from the factory maintain their quality until they are delivered to the end user. The firm's technology and its production process, which come from Switzerland and the UK, are among the best in the flour milling business.

Competition. As noted above, Takoradi Flour Mills is one of three companies now operating in the flour milling industry. The others are Irani Brothers & Others and Tema Flour Mill.

Supply and marketing chain. Wheat is imported from Canada and Europe. Originally, wheat imports were undertaken on behalf of the company by the Ghana National Procurement Agency (GNPA). (Before liberalization, GNPA was the governmental agency responsible for the procurement and import of wheat into Ghana.) The procurement of wheat by the GNPA continued until 1992. Since then, Takoradi Flour Mills has been importing its own wheat. The company currently imports about 200,000 mt of wheat annually from Canada, Europe and elsewhere. In addition to wheat, the company imports material for sacks from China.

Takoradi Flour Mills supplies all its flour products to the local market. The company deals directly with its key clients, the bakers' associations and other consumers. The company has three depots to cover the country. Customers buy the products directly from the factory or the depots. The company has its own fleets of trucks to deliver to its depots.

Exports. All the wheat flour produced by the company is sold on the local market. However, the company exports a byproduct, wheat bran, to Morocco.

Development agenda. The company envisages expanding its capacity with a view to exporting premium flour and wheat bran to other countries in the West African subregion. The company is also seeking to diversify into other lines of business.

5.2.3   Parlays Ghana Limited

Basic details. Parlays Ghana was founded in 1993 by Dayou Purswani, an Indian who has lived most of his life in Ghana and was educated at the University of Ghana, Legon. Located on the Spintex Road, in one of Accra's industrial areas, the company is the second largest biscuit manufacturer in Ghana.

The company is a family business managed by the owner and his wife. Parlays employs 200 people, of which 60% are casual workers.

History. In 1993, Dayou Purswani was the sole distributor of Burton Biscuits (one of the largest biscuit manufacturer in the UK) on the University of Ghana campus. Through the distributorship, he observed a huge untapped market and demand for biscuits in Ghana and conceived the idea of manufacturing his own line of quality biscuits.

To pursue his goal he visited India and discussed his plans with a number of manufacturers of biscuit-producing equipment. Through those visits, he acquired a set of equipment to produce biscuits in Ghana to test the market. He brought the equipment to Ghana in 1995, employed one chemist (to help ensure that the biscuit mixture was accurate), one engineer (to man and service the equipment) and a few additional staff who helped with the sealing and packaging of the biscuits. The process at that time was manual and the wrappers were sealed with hot plates. Given the manual processes, production volumes were very low: only 2 mt of biscuits per day. The trials were successful and within a few months demand for the company's biscuits grew, necessitating the purchase of additional equipment. Using a building that he inherited as collateral, he secured financing from the Ghana Leasing Company to acquire a complete biscuit production line in 1995. That same year, the company, Parlays Biscuits Ghana, was officially registered.

Current activities and products.   Parlays Biscuits manufactures 12 different kinds of biscuit: Parlays Glucose Biscuits, Parlays Digestive Biscuits, Parlays Cream Crackers, Parlays Shortbread, Parlays Gem Biscuits, Parlays Ginger Biscuits, Parlays Coconut Biscuits, Parlays Chocolate Biscuits, Petit Biscuits, Mmofra Mmofra Biscuits,[15] Glu Glu Biscuits and Malt & Milk Biscuits. These biscuits are packaged in packs of four, six and eight. The company currently produces 300 bags of biscuits a day.

As part of its marketing strategy the company uses celebrities to promote its products. Parlays biscuits became famous in Ghana when one of Ghana's most celebrated footballers, Abedi Pele, appeared on the wrappers and in the company's advertisements. This improved the company's brand image, resulting in increased sales. A similar strategy was successfully used when wrappers were branded with the name of Emmanuel Adebayor, one of Togo's best football players, for biscuits the company exported to Togo.

The production process of the company is depicted in Figure 5.3.

Organization and management.   Reporting to the board of directors is the managing director, who is also the founder of the company. He is supported by managers responsible for finance, manufacturing and administration. Departments have some degree of autonomy for decision making. Devyani Purswani, who is one of the directors of the company, manages the distribution team and wholesalers.

---

[15] Mmofra Mmofra means children in the local Akan dialect of Ghana.

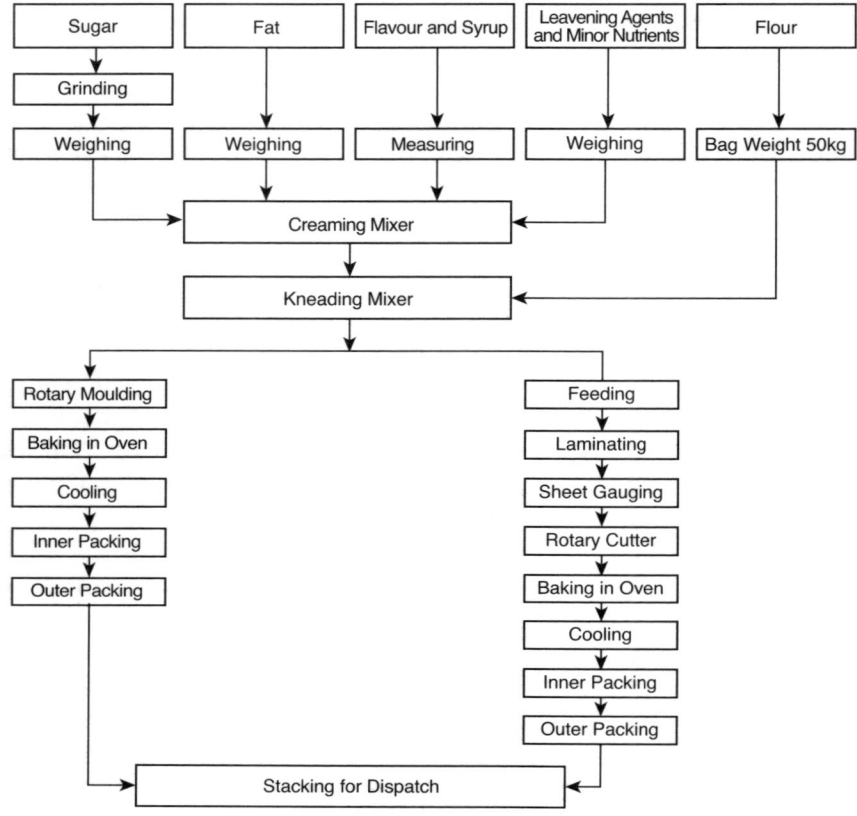

FIGURE 5.3. The production process at Parlays Ghana.
(The Parlays Biscuits Process Flow was provided by Dayou Purswani.)

Employment levels at Parlays have been falling over the years as a result of automation of the production process. The company had a staff strength of 400 about a decade ago, but this has fallen to about 200 now.

Firm capabilities. The company has a competent and dedicated team of technical and production professionals. It uses modern technology and equipment to manufacture products of different types and flavours and to ensure that it can deliver on commitments to clients. The company values feedback from traders and wholesalers and Dayou Purswani has forged a close relationship with distributors, who provide valuable market information.

Competition. Parlays faces competition from Piccadilly Biscuits, Britannica, Fairbon Biscuits and Eurofood Ghana Limited. Parlays is the second biggest producer after Piccadilly. Besides competition from local companies, there is a large variety of cheap imported biscuits on the market. The biggest challenge for the local companies is the rising cost of inputs and utilities, which erodes margins as they are unable to pass on increases in operating costs due to the presence of cheap imports.

Supply and marketing chain. Flour is imported from Turkey.

The biscuit manufacturing process begins with mixing and dough making, moulding and cutting, baking and cooling. The biscuits are then sealed and packed, after which they are sent along the supply chain to wholesalers and retailers (Figure 5.3).

All output is sold on the local market. Before the influx of foreign biscuits onto the Ghanaian market, Parlays accounted for about 55% of the biscuit market.

Parlays has a distribution network across all ten regions of the country. Distribution to retailers and consumers is undertaken by wholesalers and traders.

Exports. Three years ago, the company exported some products to Togo. The difficulties in accessing the Togolese market, as a result of import restrictions, frustrated the company's inroads into the new market. Exports were discontinued to allow the company to focus on the local market.

Development agenda. Parlays is now seeking to expand its production to improve capacity utilization. The company is also trying to strengthen its relationship with suppliers, wholesalers and consumers.

5.2.4 MV Brands (Pioneer Food Cannery Limited)

Basic details. Pioneer Food Cannery is a Free Zones company that was established in 1972. It is located at the Tema fishing harbour and it is the largest fish processing company in Ghana.

The company has a workforce of over 1,500 and a turnover of US$130 million (2010).

History. Pioneer Food Cannery was founded by a Ghanaian, Robert Ocran, as Mankoadzi Fisheries in 1972. The company started as a small factory with a production capacity of 50 mt per day, canning herring and mackerel. Robert Ocran was the first Ghanaian to undertake large-scale fishing, having migrated from fishing in small boats to trawler fishing. Prior to his involvement in fishing, he served with the Recce Regiment of the Ghana Armed Forces.

In 1994 the company was acquired by the H. J. Heinz Company Ltd. Renamed as the Pioneer Food Company, the focus was shifted from canning herring and mackerel to processing and canning tuna and tuna loins for export to the US. After the acquisition, over US$10 million was invested in the company to expand its operation to 160 mt per day. The company acquired Free Zone status in 1995.

In 2006 the European seafood division of H. J. Heinz sold its interest in Pioneer Food Cannery to the private investors MW Brands, a holding company owned by Lehman Brothers Merchant Bank with operations in France, Portugal and the Seychelles. The group also owns TTV Limited, a fishing company which supplies tuna to Pioneer Food Cannery. The company was restructured and its operational capacity increased to process over 200 mt of tuna per day.

In 2010 MW Brands sold its interest in Pioneer Food Cannery to Thai Union EU Seafoods, a company involved in the processing of tuna and shrimp.

Current activities and products. Pioneer Food Cannery produces canned tuna and frozen tuna loins for both the local and international markets. Other products include vegetable oil, brine and fresh green peppers.

Organization and management. Currently, Pioneer Food Cannery has a four-member board of directors, comprising the group CEO, the general manager, the purchasing manager and the country finance manager.

The six-member management team includes the general manager, the country finance manager, the head of operations, the head of human resources, the head of engineering and the head of quality, health safety and environment.

Firm capabilities. Pioneer Food Cannery has a processing capacity of 200 mt of tuna per day, of which 180 mt is canned tuna and 20 mt tuna loins. The company operates according to global quality and safety standards. The company has ISO 9001:2000 and ISO 14001:2004 certification and meets the British Retail Consortium global standards (BRC Grade A).

The company currently sells under a number of international brands. The John West brand is a leading canned fish brand in the UK, the Netherlands, Ireland and elsewhere. The Petit Vavires brand is the leading brand for standard tuna in France, while Mareblu is the longest-established brand in the Italian market. Other brands include Royal Pacific and Starkist.

Pioneer Food Cannery was designated the best food processing company in Ghana in 2009 and 2010.

Competition.   The only local competitor is Myroc Food Processing Group, a small Ghanaian tuna processing company that sells locally.

Supply and marketing chain.   Tuna is supplied by TTV Limited, 60% of whose annual catch of about 30,000 mt goes to Pioneer Food Cannery.

Exports.   Pioneer Food Cannery exports branded and privately labelled canned tuna to major European markets. The company supplies Marks and Spencer, Sainsbury's, Tesco, ASDA and Brakes in the UK, Leaderprice, Les Doris, System U and Carrefour in France, Mareblu and Mare D'oro in Italy, and Nixe, Sargona and Atlantic in Germany. Other export destinations include Ireland, the Netherlands, Finland, Poland, Switzerland, Cyprus, Malta and Denmark. Pioneer Food Cannery also exports to other West African countries and to Libya.

Challenges.   The main issue facing the company is competition from low-price imported canned tuna from Thailand and elsewhere. The high cost of utilities is seen as a serious problem. Pioneer Food Cannery suffers from unauthorized use of its labels on canned tuna products.

Development agenda.   Pioneer Food Cannery increased its capacity from 33,000 mt per annum in 2006 to 48,000 mt in 2010 and will further increase capacity to 55,000 mt over the next four years.

5.2.5   Unilever Ghana Limited

Basic details.   Unilever Ghana is a public company listed on the Ghana Stock Exchange. Unilever PLC owns 66.7% of its shares and the remaining 33.3% are owned by public portfolio investors, including 12,000 Ghanaians. The company has two businesses: a fast-moving consumer goods factory (located in the Tema Industrial Area); and a palm plantation called Twifo Oil Palm Plantation (located at Twifo in the Western region) that manufactures and exports crude palm oil and also supplies the Tema factory with its crude palm oil requirements.

The company has 770 employees and an annual turnover of about US$115.5 million (2010).

History.   Unilever Ghana is a subsidiary of Unilever PLC, which was founded by William Hesketh Lever in the 1890s. It employs over 500 people.

Unilever Ghana was formed in 1992 by merging two subsidiaries of Unilever PLC that already operated in Ghana: Lever Brothers Ghana Limited and UAC Ghana Limited. The latter company had roots in Ghana going back to 1931, when the United Africa Company of Gold Coast (UAC) was formed by the merger of two long-established European trading companies.

Current activities and products. Unilever Ghana produces three broad categories of products: foods, home care products and personal care products. The foods category comprises spreads, tea, savoury, oils and health and wellness. The home care category covers laundry products. The personal care category covers skin cleansing and oral products. The company's leading brands are Blue Band margarine, Lipton, Royco, Food Seasoning, Annapurna salt, Omo, Key soap, Pepsodent, Close-Up, Lux, Geisha and Sunlight.

Organization and management. The company has an 11-member board of directors. The management team, headed by the managing director, comprises the heads of human resources, finance, customer development, brand building (marketing) and supply chain (procurement). Some of the functional heads have additional responsibilities for Unilever West Africa's operations in Ivory Coast.

Firm capabilities. Unilever Ghana is an ISO 14001:2004 certified manufacturing company, with a broad range of manufacturing capabilities in fast-moving consumer goods.

Competition. The company's main local competitor is PZ Cussons Ghana. Most of its products face substantial competition from low-price imports.

Supply and marketing chain. Palm oil (supplied by Twifo Oil Palm, a subsidiary of Unilever Ghana), salt and shrimps are sourced locally.
Unilever Ghana's system of distribution, developed in 1995, makes its products accessible throughout Ghana. With 46 key distributors, it reaches over 100,000 retail, wholesale and other outlets.

Exports. The company exports to Nigeria, Kenya, South Africa and Ivory Coast.

Challenges. The high cost of funds from financial institutions, and competition from locally produced and imported substitutes, are the company's main current concerns.

Development agenda. Unilever's aim is to maintain market leadership through the introduction of innovative products.

Chapter 6

NON-ALCOHOLIC BEVERAGES

6.1   Sector Profile

Background and overview.   The non-alcoholic beverages industry in Ghana can be broken down into four sub-markets.

Carbonated drinks.   This covers drinks such as Coca Cola, Fanta, Sprite, Pepsi and Mirinda. These are normally bottled in or distributed from regional capitals and the bottles are collected and returned to the factory and refilled – and the cycle continues. A large collection of canned imported drinks also fall into this category. A subcategory comprises 'energy' drinks such as Blue Jeans, Zero, Rox, Burn, Rhino and Red Bull.

Juices.   This covers a range of concentrates and fresh juices that are either imported or produced locally. While most of the imported juices are made from concentrates, the fresh juices are produced locally as most have short shelf lives. Fresh pineapples, bananas, mangoes, guavas and oranges are the leading fruits processed into juices. The fresh juices are packaged mainly in Tetra Paks, glass bottles, polyethylene terephthalate (PET) bottles and plastic gallons. Local fresh juice producers include Papso, Milani, Aquafresh, Rush Farms, Akramang Ltd, Winfield Farms, Sunripe Ltd, Coastal Groves Ltd and Athena Foods Ltd. In addition, companies such as Blue Skies, Pinora and Athena Foods Ltd are able to supply bulk juice and chopped fruit to EU buyers.

Fruit drinks such as Ceres from South Africa and Purejoy and Don Simon from Italy are leading imported brands.

Per capita consumption of fruit juice in Ghana is estimated at 0.52 litres per year, which translates to 10.4 million litres per annum nationwide. Of this, 17% is from imports, 44% is local Tetra Pak packaged product and 39% is bottled juice.

Milk.   Locally produced fresh milk is in limited supply and is available mainly in supermarkets in Accra and Kumasi. UHT or long-life carton milk is more widely available in some regional capitals. Powdered milk in tins or plastic bags is widely available across Ghana. In view of the limited domestic livestock capacity, a large proportion of milk products are imported. Fan Milk Limited is the leading producer of dairy products in Ghana.

Water. There is a high demand for bottled and sachet water in Ghana, reflecting the high temperatures throughout the year. There are 20 companies registered by the Food and Drugs Board to produce bottled water. These companies account for about 95% of the bottled water available locally on the market. Local brands include Voltic, Dasani, Bon Aqua, Yes, Safina, Aqua Fill, Ice Cool, Ice Pak, Divine Aqua, Meridian Filtered Water, Mobile Water, Still Pure and Smile Natural Mineral Water. The leading local bottled water producers are Voltic Ghana Limited, Coca Cola Bottling Company of Ghana Limited, Ice Cool Purified Water Limited and Yes Mineral Limited. Imported brands include Vittel, Comtrex, Volvic and Evian.

The sachet water industry is in a state of flux and is highly fragmented, with over 1,800 small and medium-sized companies officially registered with the National Association of Sachet Water Producers. Registration is voluntary and about twice the registered number are not registered. With an average annual production of 2.7 million litres, the total size of the sachet water market was estimated to be about US$350 million in 2009. This represents an annual average growth rate of about 14% over the 1995 value of about US$120 million. Sachet water is normally packaged in plastic bags with a volume of 500 ml.

Structure of the industry. The Coca Cola Company and Beverage Investment Ghana Limited (also known as Pepsi Cola Ghana) are the leading companies in carbonated drinks. A second group of companies – including Guinness Ghana Breweries Limited, Accra Brewery Limited and Kasapreko Company Limited – comprises companies that are primarily producers of alcoholic beverages but have strong soft drink businesses. A third group comprises the large number of SMEs that focus on juices that rely on local fruit as input. Companies in this category include Papso, Milani, Aquafresh and Healthilife. The fourth, and final, category comprises a large number of micro and small establishments, mostly sole proprietors, that produce a large range of non-alcoholic drinks for the market. The actors in this last category are largely unregulated; most operate from home.

Supply and marketing chain. The multinationals rely on their international network to procure all their major inputs. The large local companies and SMEs in the carbonated segment procure inputs from international suppliers. Manufacturers in the juice segment rely on the supply of fresh fruits from local sources. Some buy directly from the farm gate while others subcontract supply to third parties. The local supply chain is not efficient and is fraught with problems. The most successful companies are those that are able to ensure regular supplies. Firms in the dairy segment, such as Fan Milk Limited, rely heavily on international procurement for milk powder, their main input.

Multinationals such as Coca Cola have distribution depots across the country. Several SMEs serve as wholesale distributors for the major producers.

Policy context. The industry benefits from tax incentives on imported agro-processing equipment that apply to all processors of agricultural products. The Food and Drugs Board and the Ghana Standards Board are empowered to ensure that all categories of food and drinks on the market in Ghana are duly certified as safe for human consumption. These institutions continue to take steps to improve the safety of all non-alcoholic beverages on the local market.

Challenges. Among the key issues facing the non-alcoholic beverage industry is the high cost of utilities such as electricity and water. The seasonality of production (due to the reliance on rain-fed farming practices) results in irregular supply of raw materials (fruits) throughout the year, and this undermines production schedules if producers are unable to make alternative arrangement to access fresh fruits. Lack of access to financing and the high cost of packaging are among the key constraints.

One of the biggest challenges is the disposal and management of the plastic waste from the water sachet producers. The government has imposed an additional tax on sachet water producers to mitigate the environmental issues associated with plastic waste.

Competitiveness. It is anticipated that in the next five years the industry will grow by a minimum of 10% annually in response to strong demand and the entry of new players into the market. Brands will grow stronger as marketing intensifies, with traditional soft drink producers moving into other products such as confectionery, water and fruit-flavoured drinks.

Export status, strength and potential. Ghanaian juice producers have potential export markets in the Sahel region of West Africa, where the majority of the population do not consume alcoholic beverages for religious reasons and where climatic conditions are not conducive to the cultivation of fruits. This market is currently unexploited by Ghanaian juice producers as they have yet to meet domestic demand.

Only a few companies, such as Blue Skies, Pandora and Athena Foods Ltd, are able to supply bulk juices and chopped fruits to EU buyers, given the stringent standards requirements.

Recent developments.   Changing habits and eating patterns have resulted in a gradual shift from carbonated drinks to natural fruit juices.

Large firms.

Nestlé Ghana Ltd, a subsidiary of the multinational Nestlé SA, started business in Ghana in 1957 with the importation of milk and chocolates. In 1971 it began local production with Ideal Milk and Milo. Since then the product portfolio has increased, with the production of Carnation, Carnation Tea Creamer, Chocolim, Chocomilo, Cerelac, Cerevita, Nestea, Nescafé Cream 3 in 1 and Nesquik, which is produced for export. A full profile of the company appears in the next section.

Aquafresh Limited was established as a limited liability company in 1994. The company produces natural fruit juices and drinks. Their main products are Calypso, milk, juice, Fruity and Frutelli. A full profile appears in the next section.

Guinness Ghana Breweries Limited and Ghana Breweries Limited are subsidiaries of the Guinness Ghana Breweries Group. The company was formed on 1 January 2005 as a result of a merger between Guinness Ghana Breweries Ltd and Ghana Breweries Limited. Guinness Ghana Breweries is one of the top three alcoholic and non-alcoholic beverage manufacturers in Ghana. The non-alcoholic beverage line of the company includes brand names such as Malta Guinness (a malt-based soft drink). Several competitors now offer malt-based soft drinks.

SBC Beverages Ghana Limited (Pepsi Cola) is a subsidiary of Pepsi Cola International. It is profiled in the next section.

Coca Cola Bottling Ghana is a subsidiary of the Coca Cola company. It is Ghana's largest supplier of carbonated soft drinks.

Medium-sized firms.   Among the medium-sized firms in the soft drinks industry, Papso Ghana Limited is one of the more prominent players. The company was founded in 1966 by a Ghanaian entrepreneur, Lord Asare, and it employs 28 people. The company initially produced alcoholic beverages, with two main products: Major and Kebashoo. Even though the alcoholic beverage business was profitable, Asare decided for religious reasons to change the firm's focus from alcoholic to non-alcoholic beverages.

The company originally had an orange and pineapple farm, named Rush Farms. In 2004 the farming activities were closed down and since then Papso imports fruit concentrates and flavours from South Africa. Other inputs including ginger and pineapples are sourced locally.

PAPSO Ghana Limited produces fruit juices in seven flavours, all packaged in 330 ml bottles (sourced from the open market) as well as in gallons. The company also produces bottled water.

Papso Ghana Limited now aims to export to neighbouring West African countries.

Small-scale, informal and peripheral activities. There are several small-scale producers of carbonated drinks, juices and sachet water across the country but most are heavily concentrated in the two main cities of Accra and Kumasi. Most are informal and unregulated and operate with limited market reach.

Rationale for selecting profiled firms. Nestlé Ghana Limited, Aquafresh and SBC Beverages Ghana are among the five leading producers of soft drinks.

6.2 Profiles of Major Firms

6.2.1 Nestlé Ghana Limited

Basic details. Nestlé Ghana, the leading manufacturer of beverages, has operated in Ghana for over 50 years. It employs 850 full-time staff.

History. Nestlé began its operations in Ghana in 1957 as Nestlé Products Ghana, importing chocolates. In 1969 Nestlé became a partnership between Nestlé SA (a 55% shareholding) and the National Investment Bank of Ghana (a 45% shareholding).

The company commenced production at its first factory in Ghana in 1971 to take advantage of the availability of locally produced cocoa. When the factory was commissioned, Milo and Ideal Milk were its main product lines. New product lines were introduced over time.

From Ghana, Nestlé expanded its operations into other African countries including Ivory Coast, Nigeria, Senegal, Gabon and Guinea. In 2000, Ghana became the base for Nestlé's operations in Central and West Africa.

Current activities and products. Nestlé's core products are Ideal Milk, Nido, Cerelac, Cervita, Milo, coffee and Chocolimand Ice Tea in the beverages section and Maggi seasoning in the food area.

Organization and management. Nestlé Ghana has six main departments each under a functional head (or line manager) who reports directly to a managing director. The managing director reports to the board in Switzerland.

Firm capabilities. Nestlé Ghana relies heavily on its parent company for research and development, procurement, training and capacity building and knowledge management.

Competition. Nestlé faces competition from Coca Cola, Pepsi Cola and fruit drink manufacturers.

Another source of competition is imported beverages and fruit juices such as Ceres and Purejoy, which are sometimes cheaper on the market. The company also faces competition from dairy products such as Peak Milk, which is produced in Nigeria.

Supply and marketing chain. Nestlé imports most of its inputs. Suppliers are recruited from Nestlé's headquarters in Switzerland. Finished products are sent to warehouses for onward delivery to wholesalers, distributors, retailers or vendors (sales promoters).

Nestlé has engaged a large number of vendors who get their supplies from distributors and retailers to sell at vantage spots on streets, in parks and other open spaces, and so on. This marketing strategy has enabled Nestlé to sustain its market share in an increasingly competitive industry. The vendors are supported with facilities such as coolers, mobile vending machines, coffee makers, umbrellas and small carts to help facilitate their sales.

Exports. Nestlé exports its Cerevita (a wheat-based cereal) to Nigeria, Ivory Coast and other Central African countries. Local consumption of Cerevita is low, but there is a high level of demand in the export markets. The Ghanaian market has a strong preference for an alternative product, Cerelac, which is a maize-based cereal that is slightly heavier.

Development agenda. The development agenda of Nestlé Ghana over the next five years is to expand its product range. It is also considering introducing soft drinks and bottled water to its product range.

6.2.2 Aquafresh Limited

Basic details. Aquafresh, a family business, was established as a limited liability company in 1994 under the Ghana Companies Code 1963. All three shareholders are family members and are Ghanaians of Lebanese decent.

Aquafresh employs about 100 people.

History. The story of Aquafresh starts some 50 years ago, when the father of the current board chairman established Millet Textile, a company which manufactured towels for the Ghanaian market. The firm's name was later changed to Spintex and it developed into an integrated textile firm that manufactured high-quality textiles for the Ghanaian and wider African market. Spintex, however, faced severe competition as a result of the influx of imported used clothing onto the Ghanaian market. This was as a result of the liberalization of the Ghanaian economy under the Structural Adjustment Reform Programme of the International Monetary Fund and the World Bank, which resulted in the abolition of import restrictions. Locally produced textiles could not compete with low-priced used clothing. The name of the company was changed to Printex as the company focused on the printing of African wear to set it apart from the competition. As the competition from used clothing continued to undermine the prospects of the company, the shareholders took a strategic decision to diversify their business and income sources. Aquafresh was established following a series of studies of business opportunities.

Aquafresh commenced operation with the introduction of a product called Fruity, which was promoted through an advert using the popular Ghanaian folklore character Kwaku Ananse. Even though this product caught on well in the market, production was suspended due to packaging issues. The company enhanced its packaging, rebranded and relaunched with a number of new products that went on to become household names.

Current activities and products. The Aquafresh range of drinks includes

- Kalyppo (apple, fruit mix, orange, citrus, passion, oranpine, pineapple, guava and strawberry flavours),
- Milko (chocolate flavour),
- Juicee (cocktail, orange, citrus and pineapple flavours),
- Fruity (cocktail, orange, citrus punch and pineapple flavours) and
- Frutelli (cocktail, orange, mango, citrus splash and orange/pineapple flavours).

Organization and management.   The three board members are all members of the Millet family. The managing director, Milad Millet, is assisted
by general managers for operations and administration. Other functional
heads report to the two general managers. Delegation of authority and
responsibility are highly encouraged.

Firm capabilities.   Aquafresh was one of the first Ghanaian companies
to be certified by the Foods & Drugs Board to operate under the Hazard
Analysis & Critical Control Point system to guarantee food safety, and it is
audited periodically by the Foods & Drugs Board.

Competition.   Aquafresh's leading competitors include Blue Skies, A-life
Limited, Healthilife Limited and Coca Cola Ghana Limited. Aquafresh also
faces competition from a large variety of imported fruit juices with brands
such as Ceres and Purejoy.

Supply and marketing chain.   Originally, Aquafresh sourced its fruit concentrates locally. However, there were problems with regularity of supplies
due to the inability of local farmers to meet supply schedules. Rising prices
were also a major issue. The company now sources its fruit concentrates
from China and other Asian countries.

The company has two modes of marketing: direct sales to bulk buyers
and selling via its 100 distributors across the country.

The production process at Aquafresh is illustrated in Figure 6.1.

Exports.   Aquafresh exports 15–20% of output to Burkina Faso, Togo,
Benin, Mali, Niger, Ivory Coast and Senegal. With the exception of Senegal,
where the products are exported by sea freight, delivery is by road transport.

The company faces major constraints in accessing the African francophone countries due to restrictive import policies, despite being signatories
to the Economic Trade Liberalisation Scheme under the ECOWAS Protocol.

Development agenda.   The development agenda of Aquafresh is to expand
its market reach to cover the whole of West Africa.

6.2.3   SBC Beverages Ghana Limited (Pepsi Cola)

Basic details.   SBC manufactures and distributes Pepsi Cola beverages.
SBC was set up in 1958, as part of the government of Ghana's industrial-
ization drive under the first president of the Republic of Ghana, Dr Kwame
Nkrumah. The company is located in the main industrial area of Accra.

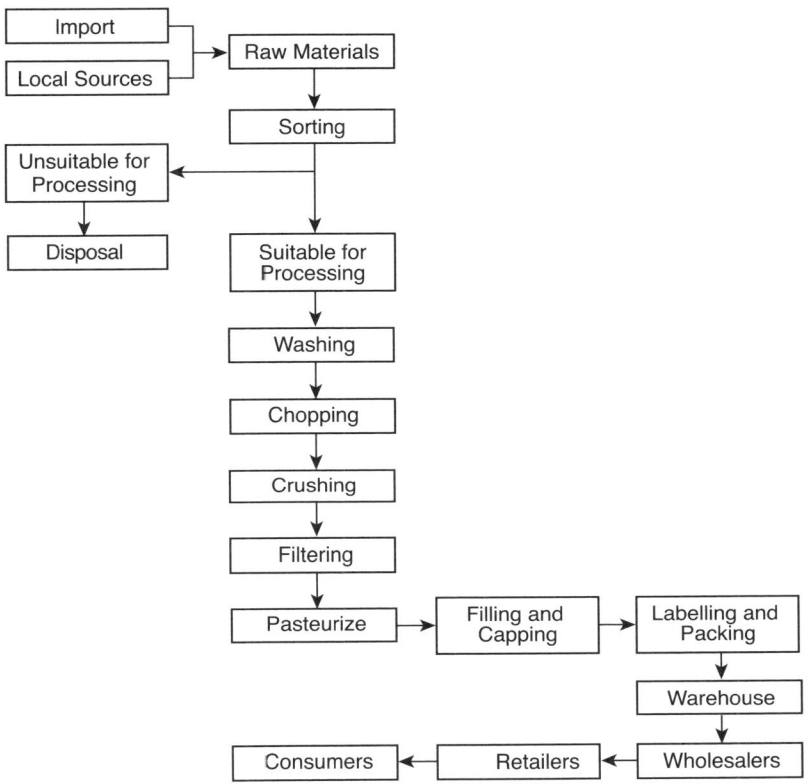

FIGURE 6.1. Aquafresh's production process.

History. The company was established in 1958 as Ghana Bottling Company, under a government directive. It became one of several industries supervised by the Ghana Industrial Holding Corporation (GIHOC), with a mandate to produce a range of Pepsi brand beverages under franchise.

In 1998, under the privatization programme of the government of Ghana, Pepsi Cola was divested. The company was taken over by a group of Ghanaian private investors who operated under the registered name of Beverage Investment Ghana Limited. Pepsi Cola International was unhappy with the company's shortcomings in meeting the standards of the brand and the franchise. In April 2008 Pepsi Cola International withdrew the franchise and awarded it to SBC International (the owners of Seven-Up Bottling Company). The new owners of the franchise renamed the company SBC Beverages Ghana. The Pepsi brand name was retained.

Current activities and products. SBC is the third largest producer/manufacturer of soft drinks and non-alcoholic beverages in Ghana after Coca Cola Bottling Ghana and Ghana Breweries Limited. The company produces three main generic brands of soft drinks, namely Mirinda, Pepsi Cola and 7UP. Mirinda comes in three different flavours: orange, pineapple and fruity. The company is due to introduce another flavour called 'soda' under the Mirinda brand later in the year.

In 2007 SBC began manufacturing Aquasplash, its brand of bottled water. The company inherited an old production plant with poor productivity but it has now reached break-even point, producing 1.2 million cases a year.

Organization and management. The managing director reports to the board of directors in Beirut, Lebanon. Line managers head the several functional areas: human resources, procurement, sales and marketing, production, finance, auditing, quality assurance and inventory.

The current total staff strength is 300, of which a third are casual employees. The company also employs part-time staff who undertake peripheral jobs such as washing of bottles, packaging and packing. These part-time staff are employed directly through daily applications received at the front desk.

Firm capabilities. Its operations in Ivory Coast and other countries in Africa and the Middle East allow SBC to move expertise across its operations to support particular facilities. The firms offers continuous training and courses for its staff and enjoys a low level of staff turnover.

Competition. SBC's main competitor is Coca Cola Bottling. Although SBC does not currently produce high volumes, due to the limitations of its plant and equipment, it aims to maintain its current market share. The forthcoming acquisition of new plant is expected to improve the competitiveness of SBC through increased production, regular supplies and the implementation of a full range of marketing and promotion strategies.

SBC's other competitors are fruit juice manufacturers such as Papso, Aquafresh, Milani, Blue Skies, etc. SBC Pepsi Cola plans to introduce a new line of fruit juices.

Supply and marketing chain. Sugar and concentrates are imported from the US and, sometimes, from China. The bottles were originally sourced locally but, due to the limited capacity of local bottling facilities, SBC currently imports bottles from India and Nigeria.

The packed products are distributed to depots across the country for onward distribution to wholesalers and retailers.

Exports.   The company does not export.

Development agenda.   The immediate objective of the company is to achieve full turnaround and achieve and maintain profitability. The five-year development plan is to acquire new plant and equipment and to relocate to a more suitable site as the current location suffers from floods during periods of heavy rain.

Chapter 7

ALCOHOLIC BEVERAGES

7.1   Sector Profile

Background and overview. It has been estimated that the annual per capita consumption of alcohol in Ghana is approximately 1.54 litres of pure alcohol.[1] Locally manufactured alcoholic drinks account for 88% of consumption, with the remaining 12% coming from imports. There are six large producers and a large number of medium-sized and small firms who together produce over 200 brands.

Structure of the industry. Ghana's alcoholic drinks industry has three segments.[2] The first comprises hard liquors such as whisky, brandy, schnapps, gin and rum. The second comprises wines, ciders and other mild alcoholic beverages. The third comprises beers and stout (Figure 7.1).

Besides the industrially brewed drinks, there is also a huge market for traditional beverages such as Pito (prepared from millet), palm wine (produced from sugary palm saps) and Akpeteshie (distilled from fermented palm sap or sugar-cane juice).[3]

Competitiveness. The high costs of local manufacturers make their products uncompetitive against imported liquors, even though the latter attract import taxes of about 40% of the invoice price. Advertising, in both print and electronic media, is notably high.

Supply and marketing chain. Companies such as Guinness Ghana Breweries and Accra Brewery Limited import their main input, malt, but source maize grits on the local market. The hard liquor manufacturers procure up to 60% of their inputs locally.

---

[1] Evans, K. 2008. National Alcohol Policy, third draft (13 May). Report prepared for the government of Ghana.

[2] Ghana Standard Industrial Classification, Phase III Report

[3] Akpeteshie is a local Ghanaian name for a home-made alcoholic spirit produced in Ghana and other West African nations by distilling palm wine or sugarcane juice. Akpeteshie is classified in the first segment along with hard liquors, while Pito is classified in the third along with beer.

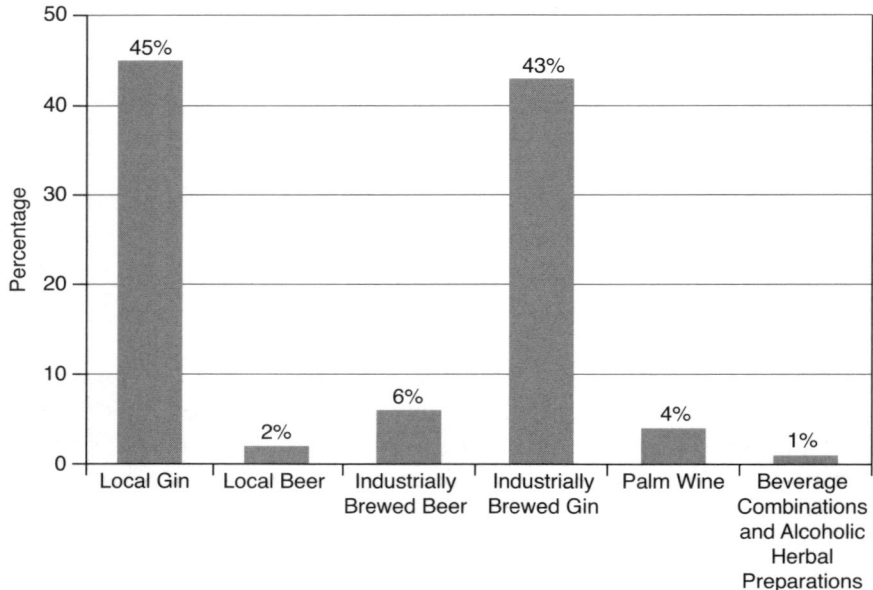

FIGURE 7.1. Consumption shares of alcoholic beverage types.

There is currently no bottle manufacturing facility in Ghana and the companies import bottles from Nigeria.

The breweries and stout manufactures have a network of third-party key distributors and a chain of depots across the country. The hard liquor manufacturers deliver directly to distributors. Retailers tend to be small and privately owned.

Policy context. The government of Ghana has drafted the National Alcohol Policy, which aims to change behaviour by encouraging positive negative patterns of consumption and discouraging negative ones, to reduce harm due to alcohol misuse, and to ensure product quality and integrity to protect consumers from unsafe products.

Challenges. The biggest issues facing the industry are the high cost of utilities (electricity and water), the high cost of inputs and increased competition from imports. Difficulties in accessing finance and the high cost of packaging have also been cited as issues affecting producers.

Profiles of selected companies. The largest companies in the industry are Accra Brewery Limited (with over 10 brands), Guinness Ghana Breweries (with Smirnoff and seven other brands), GIHOC and Kasapreko (with about a dozen different brands between them).

Accra Brewery Limited (ABL) is a subsidiary of SABMiller PLC, a leading brewer operating across six continents. ABL has been operating in the beverage industry for over 36 years and was originally known as Overseas Breweries Limited. It has been listed on the Ghana Stock Exchange since 1990. The company was incorporated on 1 April 1975 to produce beer, malt-based drinks and aerated soft drinks. Its products include Club Beer, Castle Milk Stout, Stone Lager, Club Shandy, Vitamalt, Muscatella and other brands.

ABL has a packaging capacity of between 22,000 and 36,000 bottles per hour.

Guinness Ghana Breweries, which is fully profiled below, is a subsidiary of Diageo Highlands BV, which is based in the Netherlands. (Heineken is a minority shareholder with a 20% stake.) Guinness Ghana Breweries operates three plants in Ghana: two in Kumasi (the Kaasi and Ahensan plants) and one in Accra (the Achimota plant).

Kasapreko Company Limited, which is fully profiled below, is one of the leading gin producers. It is located in Accra.

GIHOC Distilleries Company Limited, which is fully profiled below, is a government entity established by the Industrial Development Corporation in 1958 to manufacture alcoholic beverages.

Profile of a medium-sized firm.

Baron Distilleries Limited, a manufacturer of distilled and blended liquors, is the third-largest alcoholic beverage manufacturer in Ghana. Established in 1995, the company currently employs 220 workers.

Baron Distilleries began operations under the name Baronanza Enterprises as a small manufacturing entity producing one product: Baron's Lime Juice. The lime juice was developed by the company's founder Frank Sekyere, who had a background in chemistry. Sekyere started this business soon after completing his college education. The company was situated in a small wooden structure in the Airport Residential Area, a suburb of Accra. Within a year, Sekyere developed four additional products and in 1998 the company was incorporated as a limited liability company with Sekyere as sole owner. In 2000, the company moved into its current premises and has been operating there ever since.

Baron Distilleries has a sister company that manufactures purified water.

The company has ten products currently on the Ghanaian market: Baron Pusher Gin Bitters, Baron Wo Ba Ada Anaa Gin Bitters, Baron Playboy Liqueur, Baron Captains Gin, Baron Captains Whisky, Baron Chef Whisky, Baron Cargo Gin Bitters, Baron Brandy, JH Baron Aromatic Schnapps and Baron's Lime Juice.

The company sources roots and herbs locally while importing alcohol from India, flavours from France and South Africa and packaging materials from China. In 2008, the company built a new factory equipped with a fully automated rinsing, bottling and capping plant. The company aims to enter other West African countries by 2013.

7.2   Profiles of Major Firms

7.2.1   Kasapreko Company Limited

Basic details.   Kasapreko is the largest producer of alcoholic beverages in Ghana. Located in the Spintex Road area of Accra, the company has a staff strength of 130. The annual turnover of the company was US$44 million in 2010.

History.   The company was founded by Dr Kwabena Adjei, an industrialist and entrepreneur, in 1989. The company was one of several new companies, including Kantamanto, Ravico and Macbell, that set up liquor distillation businesses at about the same time in Nungua, a suburb of Accra. Before setting up Kasapreko, Dr Adjei was involved in general trading and imported a wide range of products for sale in Ghana. He was also a licensed gold buyer. (The other companies that started in the business around the same time as Kasapreko later exited the business.)

During their early years, all the companies that produced distilled products sourced inputs from the same supplier and were using the same blend to produce a generic gin. Kasapreko broke away from this tradition and sourced inputs from a different supplier to produce gin, brandy and whisky of different blends from those of its rivals. This set the company apart and enabled it to build a niche market. During this period the company operated in the informal sector.

After 10 years of operation, Dr Adjei decided to formalize the operations and systems of the company and hired professionals to review the business and put in place structures including a board, a professional management and technical team and good operational, human resources and financial management systems. This development was made possible by International Finance Corporation support for private-sector SMEs in Ghana and built on earlier entrepreneurial development support from EMPRETEC Ghana Foundation.[4] One result was a rationalization of the number of brands from about 40 to 9.

A key innovation during this time was the introduction of bitters. Though bitters (which are parts of plants) had long been used in drinks, their use in Ghana was not commercialized. Kasapreko contracted the Centre for Scientific Research into Plant Medicine to research bitters formulations and to standardize content. The centre established appropriate mixes, identified benefits, developed concentrates and standardized content. The success of this partnership between Kasapreko and the Centre for Scientific Research into Plant Medicine marked the beginning of the commercialization of bitters in Ghana.

Current activities and products. The company's brands include Alomo bitters, brandy, Cardinal liqueur, Cocoa liqueur, dry gin, Kasapak, lime cordial, Ogidigidi bitters, Opeimu bitters, tonic wine and Kasa Vino. The company uses 12 million litres of ethanol per annum.

Organization and management. The executive director reports to a board and oversees the following functional departments: production, procurement, finance, administration and marketing.

Firm capabilities. Kasapreko is the company that commercialized the operations of the informal alcoholic beverage industry in Ghana. Investment in technology has kept the company at the forefront of the sector. It is currently installing two new state-of-the-art liquor producing lines, at the cost of US$30 million, with the capacity to produce 70,000 bottles per hour.

Competition. Kasapreko's main competitors are GIHOC Distilleries and Paramount Distilleries. The company also faces competition from multinationals such as Diageo (the world's largest spirit producer), which currently imports brands such as Smirnoff, Johnnie Walker and Baileys. There are also some 400 small enterprises that produce a large range of bitters on the market, especially in Accra and Kumasi, and there is an influx of small operations from India that produce alcoholic beverages in Tetra Paks.

---

[4] EMPRETEC is a UN programme established by UNCTAD's Division of Investment and Enterprise to promote the creation of sustainable SMEs. The name EMPRETEC comes from the Spanish words for entrepreneurs ('emprendedores') and technology ('tecnología').

Supply and marketing chain.   About 80% of inputs are imported. Ethanol is imported from Brazil, India and Pakistan, flavours from the EU, bottles from China and cups/corks from India. The inputs are sourced through brokers in Europe. Inputs such as natural plants, plant parts and labels and boxes are sourced locally.

The company has key distributors and retailers in 8 of Ghana's 10 regions. It also has about six distributors in Nigeria.

Exports.   Originally, Kasapreko exported only to Ivory Coast, Burkina Faso and Nigeria but it now exports to all countries in West Africa (with Nigeria being the main destination).

Development agenda.   Kasapreko aims to extend its exports to other parts of Africa, such as Tanzania and South Africa. The company also aims to expand its sales to West African nationals living outside Africa (in London, Brussels and US states where there is a heavy concentration of people of West African origin). The company will develop technical capacity to support this expansion drive and will also consider vertical integration to improve local raw material supply.

7.2.2   GIHOC Distilleries

Basic details.   GIHOC Distilleries Company was the first modern distillery to be established in West Africa. Situated in the North Industrial Area in Accra, the company has an annual turnover of US$14 million (2010) and a total workforce of 310 employees (160 of whom are permanent staff).

History.   GIHOC Distilleries Company was established in 1958 as State Distilleries. It was one of 28 state-owned enterprises set up by the first president of Ghana, Dr Kwame Nkrumah. By the late 1980s several of these enterprises had gone into liquidation as a result of poor financial performance but GIHOC Distilleries was financially viable. Following the divestiture of the non-performing state-owned enterprises, GIHOC Distilleries was registered as a limited liability company and placed under the supervision of the Ministry of Trade and Industry, with 100% government ownership.

Current activities and products.   GIHOC Distilleries Company distils, refines, blends and produces various types of both alcoholic and non-alcoholic beverages. The company produces several brands of liquor including Lawyer London Dry Gin, Castle Bridge Gin, Buccaneer Rum, Mandingo Bitters and Herb Afrik Gin Bitters. In the non-alcoholic area, its main product is Meridian filtered water.

Organization and management.   The company is headed by a managing director appointed by the government. Line managers for administration, finance and accounts, production, marketing and sales, research and development and commercial/purchasing report to the managing director.

Firm capabilities.   The research and development department focuses on developing new formulae and blends and the company has succeeded in introducing a sequence of brands over the years.

The company has developed and maintained high quality standards as reflected by a number of awards, such as the National Quality Award (Food & Drink Sector) Ghana awarded by the Ghana Standards Board in 2002, the fifth National Indutech Award 2005 and the Ghana Star Award (Packaging) 2007.

Competition.   The company's main competitors are Kasapreko, Paramount Distilleries and Baron Distilleries. It also faces competition from multinationals such as Diageo, and from a large number of imported liquors.

Supply and marketing chain.   The company sources raw materials such as sugar, water and herbs/roots (for bitters) locally. Concentrates are imported from Spain and the UK and are produced to the company's specification. GIHOC imports bottles from Italy, while labels are sourced both locally and from abroad.

The company markets its products through key distributors across the country as well as through private wholesalers.

Exports.   GIHOC Distilleries produces products for the Nigerian market under contract. Some wholesalers export their products directly to the Nigerian market.

Challenges.   The main issue facing GIHOC Distilleries is the age of its plant and equipment, which restricts the company from expanding in response to growing demand. There is also an issue of imitation of the company's products by other distilleries. The company takes measures to protect its formulae.

Recent developments.   GIHOC Distilleries formerly relied on a local supplier for (imported) alcohol. Recently, however, GIHOC Distilleries has switched to direct importation of alcohol from Europe, enabling the company to reduce production costs.

Development agenda. GIHOC Distilleries has a five-year expansion plan to replace its plant and equipment in order to expand production capacity threefold. The company also aims to explore new export markets for its products in West Africa.

7.2.3 Guinness Ghana Breweries Limited

Basic details. Guinness Ghana Breweries is Ghana's largest beverage company. With its head office located in Achimota, Accra, Guinness Ghana Breweries operates three breweries in Ghana: two in Kumasi, at Kaasi and Ahensan, and one in Accra, at Achimota.

Guinness Ghana Breweries currently employs over 600 permanent staff along with some 400 temporary staff. The annual turnover of the company is about US$40 million.

History. Guinness Ghana Breweries was incorporated on 29 August 1960 to manufacture beer, stout and mineral water. From inception up to 2004 the company's operations focused on the importation, production, distribution and sale of Guinness Foreign Extra Stout, Malta Guinness and Gordon Spark products. In November 1990 Guinness Ghana Breweries listed provisionally on the Ghana Stock Exchange and finally had their official listing on 23 August 1991.

In 2004 Guinness Ghana Limited acquired Ghana Breweries Limited, then owned by Heineken International BV. Guinness Ghana Limited subsequently changed its name to Guinness Ghana Breweries. The acquisition added a number of premium lager brands to the original portfolio (ABC, Star and Gulder). In September 2009 Guinness Ghana Breweries, by then a subsidiary of Diageo PLC, expanded its operations to include the importation, distribution, sale and marketing of the Diageo spirits range.

Diageo, the parent company, currently owns 51% of the company's shares with Heineken owning 20%. The Social Security and National Insurance Trust is also a significant shareholder.

Current activities and products. Guinness Ghana Breweries works from two operational sites: Kaasi (Kumasi, Ashanti region) and Achimota (in the Greater Accra region). A third site in Ahensan (Kumasi) provides warehousing. The Kaasi site delivers some 45% of the annual production of Guinness Ghana Breweries and the Achimota brewery produces the remaining 55%. There are ongoing capacity expansion projects at both sites.

The main products of Guinness Ghana Breweries are

- stouts (Guinness Foreign Extra Stout),
- lagers (Star Lager Beer, Gulder Lager Beer, Heineken Lager Beer),
- adult premium non-alcoholic drinks (Malta Guinness, Amstel Malta, Alvaro (which comes in pear, pineapple and passion fruit variants)) and
- spirits (Johnnie Walker (Red, Black, Green, Gold, Blue and King James), Smirnoff Vodka (Red and Black plus flavoured varieties), Baileys Irish Cream, Captain Morgan Rum, Gordon's Dry Gin and Gilbeys Gin).

The company sold a total of 17 million cases of its assorted products to the market in the 2011 financial year.

Organization and management. Guinness Ghana Breweries has an 11-member board of directors and an executive management committee comprising the managing director, the finance director, the supply director, legal counsel, the human resources director, the corporate relations director, the marketing director and the sales director.

Competition. The main competitors of Guinness Ghana Breweries are Coca Cola, ABL, Kasapreko and GIHOC Distilleries.

Supply and marketing chain. Guinness Ghana Breweries imports malt, sugar and a number of other ingredients from Europe.

The company's products are transported from the breweries to key distributors nationwide, and these distributors sell to wholesalers and retailers. In some cases, final consumers may buy directly from the key distributors.

Development agenda. Guinness Ghana Breweries has recently embarked on several initiatives including the commissioning of two new fermentation vessels and the overhaul of the company's steam boilers and some production lines at its plant in Accra. The company is also aiming to modify its capital structure and reduce its finance cost burden.

Chapter 8

TEXTILES AND GARMENTS

8.1 Sector Profile

Background and overview. In the 1970s the textile industry employed about 25,000 workers, accounted for 27% of manufacturing employment and operated above 60% capacity.[1] The industry thrived using imported quality materials and designs and had successful brands that sold well on the local market as well as in other West African markets.

By 1975, there were 14 textile companies and some 138 medium and large-scale garment factories in the country. However, by 1982, a shortage of the foreign exchange needed to import raw materials resulted in a decline in output and the eventual closure of most of the factories – both publicly and privately owned ones. These developments were widely attributed to the trade liberalization reforms that came in as part of the Structural Adjustment Programmes pursued by the government in the 1980s and 1990s.

As of 2002, four companies survived: Ghana Textile Manufacturing Company, Akosombo Textiles Limited (ATL), Ghana Textile Printing Company Limited (GTP) and Printex. Over the past five years, the industry has gone through another difficult phase as a result of competition from imported textiles and garments. This led to the shutting down of production lines and widespread redundancies. GTP shut down its spinning and weaving departments and laid off workers, while Ghana Textile Manufacturing Company shut down its production line altogether in 2005.

Textiles. Ghana's textile industry produces fabrics for the local garment industry and for the export market. The industry is predominantly cotton-based, producing African prints (wax, Java, fancy, bed sheets and school uniforms) and household fabrics (curtain materials, kitchen napkins, diapers and towels). These products form the bulk of output. Man-made fibres (synthetics) play a smaller role but are used in products such as uniforms,

[1] Ministry of Trade and Industry (2004).

knitted blouses and socks. A number of small firms print their own designs by hand onto bleached cotton fabrics (known as tie-and-dye or batik cloth).

Local textiles. Kente is a brilliantly colourful fabric, entirely handwoven by Ghanaian weavers. The brilliant colours and intricate designs associated with kente have definitely made this fabric the best known of all Ghanaian, and perhaps even all West African, textiles. Every design carries a story with a traditional meaning, giving each cloth its own distinct identity. Kente is usually worn for ceremonies, festivals and special functions such as weddings, child naming ceremonies and graduations.

Adinkra is a highly valued hand-printed and hand-embroidered cloth. Its origins can be traced back to the Asante people of Ghana and the Gyaman people of Ivory Coast. Around the nineteenth century the Asante people developed their unique art of adinkra printing. Adinkra cloth is used for a wide range of social activities and special occasions such as festivals, weddings, naming ceremonies, etc. Through innovations, local designers use adinkra symbols in the creation of a wide range of products, including clothing accessories, interior decorations, packaging and book covers.

Batik and tie-and-dye are methods of dyeing and printing cloth originally popularized in West Africa, especially among the Hausas of northern Ghana and Nigeria. Cloths are tied, either with string or rubber bands, into some sort of pattern and then dyed, either by submerging them or by squirting dye solution onto them. Where the fabric is tied, some areas do not absorb dye, thus forming a pattern.

Structure of the industry. Ghana's garment industry has two distinct products: Afrocentric and standard. Afrocentric, or traditional African, clothing is made to local design and fashion and is produced by many small enterprises, tailoring shops and seamstresses. The cloth used for these standard garments is usually imported. Companies operating in the 'standard' category seek to produce large volumes of specific garments such as shirts or trousers for export.

Traditional African clothing began as a trend in the 1980s when fashion designers such as Kofi Ansah designed clothing from traditional cloths such as batiks, tie-and-dye, handwoven cloths (kente) and hand-printed fabrics. These were created for the high-end clothing market and custom made to order.

The growth of the Afrocentric subsector was a response to demand from high-income Ghanaians, which attracted a new wave of designers into the industry. By the mid 1990s, exports of Ghana's traditional African wear had become an important foreign exchange earner. They are currently one of the leading non-traditional exports of the country.[2] Traditional African wear has become an important part of the country's tourism industry, with garments being promoted at international trade shows.

There have been several attempts to redevelop a 'standard' garment subsector in Ghana to take advantage of the African Growth and Opportunity Act (AGOA).[3] The impact of government intervention programmes such as the PSI on Textiles and Garments is yet to effect a revival of the sector.

Large volumes of used clothing are imported from Europe and the US. Several small and medium-sized used-clothing retailers and dealers account for about 30% of the workforce in the industry.

A textile manufacturing cluster: Bonwire kente weavers.   Kente is woven in the Ashanti and Volta regions. A cluster of weavers can be found in the Bonwire district of Ashanti[4] and in the Agotime Agbenyinase area in the Volta region: this cluster forms the Gator Kente Weaving Industry.

The Bonwire cluster involves more than 100 people. The weaving apparatus is handmade by the weavers themselves or by others who specialize in equipment making. The yarns used for weaving kente come in a variety of forms and qualities. Various colours of yarns may be combined to reflect the symbolic significance of the cloth. Silk yarns are the most prestigious. With an average strip width of four inches, several strips are carefully arranged and sewn together by hand (although some weavers now use sewing machines) to obtain the desired size.

Kente is marketed by middlemen who buy from the villages. Kente fabrics are also sold during kente festivals, which attract people from all over the country and from abroad.

A lack of managerial expertise, an absence of basic services and infrastructure such as electricity, low knowledge and skills levels, and poor packaging and marketing are among the main issues facing the clusters.

The cluster aims to organize the weavers into credit unions to improve access to finance, so expanding their operations. The cluster also aims to promote training to ensure that skills are transferred to the next generation.

Supply and marketing chain.   The industry imports dye and other chemicals, calico, khaki fabric, prints, accessories (zippers, fasteners, etc.) as well

---

[2] Non-traditional exports include products in the following subsectors: agricultural products (fresh pineapples, fresh yams, pawpaw, banana, fresh peppers/chillies, fish and sea food, cocoa waste, robusta coffee, cashew nuts, shea nuts and raw cotton), manufacturing and handicrafts.

[3] Under the AGOA, the US government offers preferential access to American markets by weak nations for the period prior to the WTO rules on free trade and competition coming into force.

[4] It is said that kente was invented in Bonwire around 1690.

as equipment and machinery from the Netherlands, China, India, the US and the EU. Cotton is sourced from Nigeria, Ivory Coast and South East Asia.

The retail sector has been expanding rapidly in recent years, with a proliferation of (high-price) boutiques alongside the opening of large-scale clothing retailers such as Woolworths (which entered the Ghanaian market in 2005).

A large number of retail outlets and shops specialize in local African wear. While some are outlets of the manufacturers, most are independent outlets that have contributed immensely to the growth and penetration of traditional African wear in Ghana.

Afrocentric clothing is sold in niche markets – the most important being African American communities in the US – and in the (relatively small) 'ethnic' market in Europe.

Policy context. The government has initiated various programmes to transform the industry to take full advantage of the AGOA and other export opportunities. Specific policies include the following.

A textile/garment cluster network. A network has been formed by the government in collaboration with the United Nations Industrial Development Organization to bring together micro, small and medium-scale operators in the textile industry. Since its inception, the cluster has assisted in training in mass-production strategies, subcontracting, and upgrading the technical, marketing and managerial skills of members.

Tariffs. The current tariff structure is being revised. It has been proposed that import duties on all imported clothing should be increased to create a level playing field for all textile products. In addition, tariffs on raw materials are to attract zero rates.

Export Action Programme on Textiles and Garments. This is a special programme under the PSI on Textiles and Garment that is designed to enhance private-sector growth and development.

New administrative procedures. New administrative procedures for importing printed textiles into the country have been introduced. Takoradi port has been named as the single point of entry for textile imports, and all goods will be physically examined by the Customs, Excise and Preventive Service.

The Economic Intelligence Task Force. The Economic Intelligence Task Force, comprising the security services and public- and private-sector institutions, has been set up to investigate cases of malpractice.

Challenges. The high cost of inputs and competition from imported garments (including used clothing) are the leading issues facing the industry. The influx of imported textiles, some of which infringe local brands, is a major concern. Limited access to finance also remains a serious challenge to local companies.

Competitiveness. Locally produced materials face stiff competition from finished imported textile prints such as calico, grey baft and furnishing materials, which usually come from Ivory Coast, Nigeria, China and, most recently, India and Pakistan. Although the locally produced finished fabrics are often better in terms of quality, the market for imported products has increased because the products have attractive colours, new designs and a softer and glossier finish. Products of various kinds – such as dresses, bed sheets, blankets, clothing, curtains, etc. – imported from countries like China are also a major source of competition to local companies.

Export status, strength and potential. The main export destinations for textiles made in Ghana are EU countries (55%), the US (25%) and ECOWAS (15%). Much of the remaining 5% is exported to South Africa, Zimbabwe, Namibia and Ethiopia. Textile and garment exports from Ghana comprise fancy prints, wax prints, Java prints, calico smocks, ladies dresses and menswear. Indigenous textile products including kente, adinkra (handprints) and fugu (a Ghanaian smock) are also exported.

Recent developments. The PSI has worked in conjunction with the Ministry for Trade and Industry to formulate strategies such as credit lines for the micro- and medium-sized companies in the industry. A new Belin Textiles International Limited plant is a Ghana–Mauritius partnership venture aimed at exporting garments to the US under the AGOA initiative. The government has also begun to take steps towards banning the import of used clothing over time.

Rationale for selecting profiled firms. Tex Styles Ghana Limited is classified as the leading textile manufacturer. ATL and Printex are two of the other three companies currently in operation.

8.2   Profiles of Major Firms

8.2.1   *Tex Styles Ghana Limited*

Basic details. Tex Styles Ghana, formerly Ghana Textile Printing Company Limited (GTP), is located in Tema, near Accra. The company employs 874 people, 11–12% of whom are casual staff. The company has an annual turnover of approximately US$48 million.

History. Tex Styles Ghana was an initiative under the industrialization strategy of the first president of Ghana, Dr Kwame Nkrumah. Prior to this, all the African prints on the Ghanaian market were imported from the Netherlands from the Vlisco Group of companies via its distributor in Ghana, Unilever (then known as UAC Ghana Limited). As a result of Dr Nkrumah's drive to set up a local manufacturer of African prints, the government contacted Gamma Holding (Vlisco's head office in the Netherlands), which led to an agreement among the three parties: Gamma Holding, Unilever PLC (UK) and the government of Ghana. This paved the way for the incorporation of GTP in 1966.

Between 1966 and 1982, GTP produced wax prints locally and imported Vlisco from the Netherlands for the Ghanaian market. With the onset of Ghana's revolution in 1982, the company suffered a severe decline in production. GTP began making losses and the foreign stakeholders, Gamma Holding and Unilever PLC, decided to lay off workers. Workers embarked on demonstrations and industrial action, driving the management out of office to be replaced by a Workers' Defence Committee – a pattern that was widespread throughout the country.

In 1992, Gamma Holding and Unilever PLC were recalled by the newly elected government of Ghana to take over the affairs of the company and, in 1994, the two foreign stakeholders began full restructuring. By the end of 1994, the shareholding structure of the company had changed to 71% Gamma Holding, 13% Unilever, 16% the Ghanaian government. Unilever disposed of its shares to a Chinese company, Trubrook, in 2004 but retained a role in helping to restructure the company. The company's name was changed in 2004 to Tex Styles Ghana Limited. In 2010, Gamma Holding sold its shares to ACTIS (an emerging-markets private equity investor), who are the current majority shareholders.

Despite the name change to Tex Styles Ghana Limited, the products of the company continue to be referred to as GTP on the market.

Current activities and products. The core business of Tex Styles Ghana is the local production of wax prints and the importation of Vlisco brand fabrics for distribution throughout the country. Currently, Tex Styles Ghana is the only distributor of the Vlisco brand in Ghana. The company is one of three companies in the Vlisco Group, the others being Vlisco Holland and Uniwax in Ivory Coast.

The wax prints have four main designs: Safoa, Adepa, Nsroma and Nustyle. These products are targeted at different segments of the Ghanaian market, and are for different occasions. The Vlisco brand of fabrics distributed by Tex Styles Ghana has been on the Ghanaian market for some 50 years. A third product is Woodin, a versatile fabric that can be sewn into clothes, upholstery, curtains and other decorative pieces. It is widely sold throughout West Africa.

Organization and management. The company has a nine-member board of directors made up of representatives of the three shareholders (ACTIS, Trubrook and the government of Ghana), the managing director and five directors of the company. The chairman of the board is also the chairman of the Vlisco Group.

Five directors oversee the sales, marketing, technical, finance and human resources departments. The director for Woodin, who is not on the board, oversees the outlets/retail stores throughout the country as well as the designers of ready-made Woodin clothing.

Firm capabilities. As one of the country's largest textiles manufacturers and with a presence in the industry for 50 years, Tex Styles Ghana represents a strong brand that is well known to Ghanaians. A constant flow of new designs and collections has been key to the firm's survival.

In 2008, Tex Styles Ghana achieved its highest production level of 16 million bales, although production has now dropped to about 8 million bales per annum. Tex Styles Ghana uses the same machinery and technology that it installed in 1966 but it has now begun to replace and upgrade plant and equipment. Its current technology is limited to the production of wax prints only.

Competition. The company faces competition from ATL and Printex, as well as from imported textiles. The firm's biggest concern relates to the copying of the company's designs by foreign textile companies.

Supply and marketing chain. Tex Styles Ghana imports grey baft from China and dye stuffs and wax from Germany and the Netherlands. Copper plates for designs are imported from other parts of Europe.

The company's concepts and designs are created in close conjunction with consumers, and the marketing department builds awareness through new product launches.

Tex Styles Ghana has depots located in Accra, Tema, Kumasi, Koforidua, Akim Oda, Cape Coast, Swedru, Takoradi, Dunkwa, Techiman, Sunyani, Bolga and Tamale. These outlets sell directly to retailers and registered distributors.

Exports.   Tex Styles Ghana exports wax prints to Togo, Benin, Burkina Faso and Calabar (Nigeria). The company also exports Woodin fabric to the US and South Africa. Wax prints are exported through distributors.

Challenges.   The main issue facing Tex Styles Ghana relates to the influx of low-priced imported textiles. Trade sanctions in Nigeria and elsewhere limit its current export potential.

Recent developments.   The company's current restructuring has improved its operations. Capital investment is enabling the company to acquire new technology and machinery.

Development agenda.   Tex Styles Ghana now aims to expand its production. The company's longer-term aim is to open factories in other African countries.

8.2.2   *Akosombo Textiles Limited (ATL)*

Basic details.   ATL is a member of the CHA Group ('CHA' is taken from the name of the founder of the group: Cha) of companies, a leading multinational textile group. The company is the largest producer of textile prints in Ghana and has a workforce of 1,450 employees.

History.   ATL was established by a Chinese entrepreneur, Cha Chi Ming, the owner of CHA Holdings, a pioneering company in the Chinese textiles industry. The company produces wax and fancy prints in Ghana.

The siting of the factory at Akosombo on the Volta Lake (on the Volta River near the Akosombo hydroelectric dam) gave it good access to water and electricity, its two major inputs.

ATL was 100% privately owned until 1979. In 1979, the government required all foreign-owned private companies in Ghana to have Ghanaian partners. In response to this, ATL sold some of its shares to two private Ghanaian entrepreneurs; Frimpong Ansah (Angelina Textiles) and Deborah Espocitto. ATL's shares are currently held by Ming (73.5%), Frimpong Ansah (20%) and Deborah Espocitto (6.5%).

Current activities and products.   ATL produces real wax and fancy prints for the local market and for export. The company's wax designs include indigo wax prints (blue and white), sepia wax block prints (that come in various base colours) and cracko wax prints (dark waxes). In the fancy (Java) prints group, the designs include double print, black and white, black (brisi) and black and brown prints, which are mostly used for funerals.

There are also the coloured fancy range of prints, comprising the classical and superior prints. Others include the traditional prints and seersucker.

Since 2004 the company has moved from volume production to high-margin products. In line with this new strategy, it has introduced high-margin wax prints (ABC, Prestige, Damax and Superwax) and high-margin fancy prints (Da Viva, Inspiration and Treasure). The Da Viva brand has two categories: ordinary and gold. Treasure uses kente motifs. Premium fancy is printed on wax cloth. In addition to these lines, the company also produces prints for institutions, churches, schools and other organizations.

Organization and management. ATL has an eight-member board of directors. The chairman of the board represents the Chinese majority shareholder, who is also the chairman of the CHA Group.

The management team comprises the executive director, the general manager, the assistant general manager, the financial controller, the sales and marketing director, the administrative director and the chief engineer.

Of the company's 1,314 employees, 24 are expatriate staff.

Firm capabilities. ATL undertakes spinning, weaving, printing and dyeing of yarn. ATL produces grey baft locally from cotton purchased from the Northern region of Ghana as well as from Burkina Faso and Ivory Coast. The company uses a unique technology developed from a blend of British, Chinese, Ghanaian and Congolese technology and expertise that it has customized, allowing it to print unique designs on wax and fancy prints.

Competition. ATL's main competitors are GTP and Printex. In addition to these local manufacturers, the company also faces competition from a large range of imported fabrics.

Supply and marketing chain. The main raw materials of the company are cotton, wax, dye and chemicals and sizing materials (i.e. cassava starch and salt). The company uses suppliers to source domestic cotton, which is produced in the northern part of the country. Wax and dye are imported from China and Europe. Chemicals are imported directly, or through suppliers. The company imports a large range of spare parts (e.g. copper rollers and screens) from China and Europe to maintain its plant and equipment.

The company sells through its associate company, CTD Textiles, as well as other major distributors. CTD Textiles is part of the CHA Group, which was set up to provide it with a distribution system. There are five distribution centres located in Kumasi, Cape Coast, Takoradi, Bolga and Accra (where the company also has its main depot). All products are sold through CTD

Textiles except for the Da Viva fancy prints, which are sold through a different distribution unit: DV Fashions.

Exports.   ATL exports to Togo, Benin, Ivory Coast, Niger, Burkina Faso, Senegal, Guinea, Nigeria and the UK.

Challenges.   Over the past decade the textile industry in Ghana has suffered from the inflow of imported fabrics. Copying of designs by both local and foreign competitors constitutes a major problem for the company.

  The volatile prices of primary cotton is a continuing problem, and this is exacerbated by scarcities following bad harvests.

Recent developments.   The company's shift in 2004 from volume production to more focused brand-based production has helped the company to strengthen its position in the market. The relocation of the ABC wax factory from Manchester in the UK to Ghana has reduced production costs for its premium wax print.

Development agenda.   The development agenda of ATL is to strengthen its brands in the Ghanaian and West African markets.

8.2.3   Printex

Basic details.   Printex is a privately owned Ghanaian company located on the Spintex Road in the Greater Accra region. It employs 600 people.

History.   The company was founded by Milad Millet as Millet Textile Corporation Limited in 1950. He was the first managing director of the company. The company was originally established to manufacture towels. In the early 1980s, the company changed its name to Spintex Limited and began to focus on spinning, weaving and the processing of furnishings, suiting and shirting materials.

  The name of the company was changed to Printex in 1997 following a modernization and expansion programme. The company's operation began with the production of black and white prints and slowly expanded with innovative designs and brands, many of which have become household names in Ghana.

  Presently, the company offers over 20 different ranges of prints.

Current activities and products.   Printex manufactures a wide range of designs and brands. These include oheneba, piesie, diamond (plain and coloured), gold print, super diamond and opanyin. Other designs and brands include ammamre, soso, egudie, exotic, fancy, adinkra, osikani, ruby, shining seersucker, ntamapa royale and super fancy. The names of the designs and brands have been chosen to resonate with their respective target markets.

In addition to its core textile brands, Printex has diversified into the production of shirting prints, shirts and stripes, suiting–shirting, drill, shirting poly (100%), shirting colour and school uniforms.

Organization and management.   The managing director, who reports to a board of directors, is responsible for the day-to-day management of the company. Functional managers include the sales manager, the production manager and the chief engineer.

Firm capabilities.   Printex has a complete set of textile manufacturing equipment and produces black and white and coloured textiles. One of the core capabilities of the company is the technical capacity to turn around products from design through processing to finished products faster than any other firm in the industry. Printex is the only textile manufacturer in Ghana that accepts designs from clients for customized products.

Staff retention is high, with average tenure exceeding 10 years.

Competition.   The firm's direct competitors are GTP and ATL. Ghana Textile Manufacturing Company and Tema Textile Limited also operate in the industry. The competitive advantage of Printex comes from its innovative designs, technical expertise, short turnaround and quality products. The diversification of the company into shirting prints, suiting and shirting materials and fabrics allows it to spread its market risk and achieve better financial results. The company currently faces substantial competition from imported textiles.

Supply and marketing chain.   Cotton, dyes and chemicals are imported from France, Germany and China.

Distribution within the Greater Accra region is by the company's own trucks. For other destinations, delivery (to wholesalers and dealers) is outsourced to third-party transporters.

Exports.   The company exports its products to Ivory Coast, Mali, Nigeria, Benin, Togo, Burkina Faso, Gambia, Niger, Angola, South Africa and Zambia.

Development agenda.   Presently, the company operates at only 60% of full capacity as a result of the influx of cheap (and pirated) imports. Enforcement of policies curtailing smuggling would allow the company to increase its output substantially.

Chapter 9

WOOD AND WOOD PRODUCTS

9.1   Sector Profile

Background and overview.   Forests cover about a third of Ghana's total area. Commercial forestry is concentrated in the southern half of the country. Accounting for 4.0% of GDP, the timber industry is the country's third-largest foreign exchange earner (Table 9.1) and it employs some 100,000 people.[1] The market is dominated by the informal sector, which accounts for 53% of local supply. This is followed by imports (34%) and the formal sector (13%).[2]

Structure of the industry.   The wood industry has not undergone any major transformations over the past two decades. By the early 1990s there were approximately 220 lumber processors in Ghana. Currently, there are about 100 sawmills in the country with 17 involved in sliced and rotary veneer. About 40 of these sawmills produce mouldings, profiles and machined wood. Six firms specialize in flooring products and doors while 10 are involved in plywood processing. The downstream segment of the wood industry (furniture production) is dominated by small enterprises that lack the capacity to produce export-grade furniture or to achieve the large volumes required to serve international markets (Table 9.2).

The formal sector produces a wide range of wood products, such as lumber (kiln or air dried), sliced veneer, plywood, rotary veneer, mouldings, flooring, boules and furniture parts for export. Only a small fraction of its products are sold on the local market.

Ghana's plantation history dates back to the 1930s, when a commercial plantation development based on a Taungya system (introduced from Myanmar) employed farmers to plant food crops in degraded forest

---

[1] FRSG. 2004. *Review Of Ghana's Forest Fiscal Regime: Comprehensive Reform Proposals.*
[2] Hamilton Resources and Consulting (Accra). 2008. *Alternative Tenure and Enterprise Models in Ghana: A Country-Level Study.*

TABLE 9.1. Foreign exchange earned from wood exports, 2000–9.

Year	Value (millions of US$)
2000	175
2001	169
2002	183
2003	174
2004	212
2005	227
2006	207
2007	249
2008	317
2009	180

Source: Bank of Ghana/Ghana Export Promotion Council.

TABLE 9.2. The number of companies involved in wood processing.

Category	Activities	Number of firms
Primary	Logging	250
Secondary	Air-dried lumber	153
	Kiln-dried lumber	71
	Ply-milling	15
	Sliced veneer	19
	Rotary veneer	18
	Treated poles	3
Tertiary	Furniture	53
	Particle boards	2
	Flooring	10
	Doors	8
	Moldings	45
	Toys	5
	Small-scale carpentry	300

Source: Ghana Investment Promotion Council.

reserves while also planting and maintaining tree saplings over a three-year tenure period. Over the past two decades, the Forestry Commission has had a target of planting 15,000 hectares annually under a programme to reforest a total of 400,000 hectares of degraded forest reserves through Taungya. This programme was not very successful: only 2,500 hectares per annum have been planted.

While most of the products of the formal sector are targeted at the export market, there is a large local market for furniture products and building materials that relies on local companies. Dominated by over 41,000 small and medium-sized carpentry establishments, the industry has seen an increase in imports of furniture from Asia generally and especially from China.

Supply and marketing chain.   About three million cubic metres of annual raw wood output provides the input for the formal and informal sectors of the industry. The biggest challenge is the low recovery rate, leading to waste and the loss of almost 70% of the raw material base. The current annual usage has been declared unsustainable. Once harvested, the timber is sent to processing facilities, most of which are located within the forest zone. Once processed, export products are transferred to ports for shipment while those aimed at the local market are transported by middlemen to various local wood markets.

The biggest sources of local demand for wood are the furniture and construction industries, which account for 75% and 24%, respectively, of the market. The furniture industry satisfies a large demand from the growing middle class, while the flourishing construction industry satisfies a steady demand for wood for housing and commercial developments. Local furniture is largely made from mixed materials, with lower durability. Imported furniture, mostly from China, currently sells at lower prices than locally produced furniture and is better finished: it is therefore now crowding out local manufacturers.

Policy context.   Over the last 15–20 years there have been efforts by the government to develop and implement policies on forest plantations to reverse the depletion of forest resources. The policies implemented include a ban on the export of round logs; an attempt in 1995 to privatize plantations; the conversion of Subri plantation into high-biodiversity natural forest; the Forest Plantation Development Fund; and the Heavily Indebted Poor Country plantation operation. There have been several policies formulated in the broad areas of wood/timber export procedures and wood/timber conservation. Most of these policies have yet to make a significant impact on the industry. Other policy interventions include the following.

Investment policy.   In the mid 1980s, the Ministry of Lands and Forestry, in collaboration with the Bank of Ghana, managed a process under which timber firms reinvested and retooled through offshore credits that were guaranteed by 30% retention of the export value in external accounts.

The Ghana Investment Promotion Centre Act 1994 (Act 478) makes provision for the automatic award of investment incentives and benefits without prior approval. These incentives include

- exemption from customs import duties on plant and machinery, equipment and accessories imported exclusively for establishing enterprises;
- depreciation or capital allowances of 50% in the year of investment and 25% in subsequent years for plant and machinery, respectively, and 20% in the first year and 10% in subsequent years for building;
- corporate tax rebates of 40–75%; and
- investment allowances of 7.5% per annum.

There are also special incentives for investing in commercial forest plantations. These include customs duty exemptions on the importation of special equipment and rebates for companies outside Accra and Tema. Additional incentives for developing and operating Export Processing Zones are provided by the Free Zones Act of 1995.

Export trade documentation.   Compliance with the Bills of Entry requirements of the Customs, Excise and Preventive Service (CEPS) and the port inspection procedures for wood exports of the Timber Industry Development Division involves a duplication of procedures. A one-step procedure would be more attractive, but this would require a higher level of technical proficiency among CEPS staff.

Import procedures.   The Ministry of Trade and Industry and the CEPS have streamlined general import procedures in response to complaints from importers and re-exporters dating back to the late 1990s. However, customs duty drawback procedures, which have a strong influence on tertiary processors' short-term cash flow, have remained a problem and the processes involved can take up to six months.

Challenges.   The most important issue facing the industry is deforestation and the erosion of the input base of the industry. According to the Country Environmental Assessment, the total forest area of Ghana decreased from 509 km^2 in 1934 to 108 km^2 in 2000: a loss of 401 km^2 in 66 years. Deforestation is happening at a pace of 65,000 hectares per year.[3] Analysts predict that if this trend is not reversed, the resource input of the wood and wood processing industry will be depleted within 20 years.

---

[3] Ghana Country Environmental Assessment 2007. World Bank.

The industry also suffers from old and inefficient plant and machinery. The industry has a very low conversion rate in sawmills: just 36% on average, although the best firms achieve rates of around 70%.[4] Firms in the informal sector lack capital and technical capacity and they have limited access to long-term finance. Most mills are not equipped for downstream processing, and wood products in the informal sector are of poor quality. The prevalence of trade in illegally cut timber on the local market remains a challenge. According to analysts, the banning of illegal timber products by the EU in 2008 and programmes such as the Voluntary Partnership Agreement of the EU have contributed to a reduction in the illegal timber trade.

The influx of cheap furniture products from Asia, and especially from China, has resulted in the closure of some medium-sized furniture companies and a large number of small enterprises.

Competitiveness. Ghana has been successful in creating an international market for semi-finished wood and wood products that serve as inputs for the furniture and construction industries in destination markets. Some large companies such as John Bitar, Naja David, Samartex and Mondial produce top-quality wood products that are in high demand internationally. However, the industry has not been competitive in the downstream finished-products markets (furniture).

Export status, strength and potential. A significant proportion of wood products from the formal sector are exported. In 2009, Ghana exported a total of 33.8 million cubic metres of wood with a value of US$14 million. The main exports are lumber (air dried), curls veneer, sliced veneer and rotary veneer.

Africa is the leading market for exports, accounting for over 40% of total exports. Four-fifths of this went to the West African subregion, with Nigeria being the biggest single market. Europe ranks second, accounting for about 30% of exports. The key markets in Europe are Italy, France, Germany, the UK, Belgium, Spain, Ireland and the Netherlands. The Asian market, dominated by India, Malaysia, Taiwan, China, Singapore and Thailand, accounted for 18% of Ghana's exports in 2009, the US accounted for 6%, and the Middle East took up the remaining 4%.[5]

---

[4] Birikorang, G. 2001. *Ghana Wood Industry and Log Export Ban Study.* Accra: Forest Sector Development Project, Forestry Commission.

Bureau of Integrated Rural Development. 2005. *Reducing Wood Waste in the Timber Industry by Strengthening Institutional Links with Wood-Based Industries: Final Report.* Accra: Ghana Land and Forest Policy Support Facility.

[5] Timber Industry Development Division. 2009. *Report on Export of Wood Products, Ghana.*

The global recession is currently affecting export volumes, which fell almost 20% from 2008 to 2009.

Recent developments.   Consumer countries have recently taken measures to exclude illegal timber products. These policies aim to reverse illegal logging in export countries. In Europe and the US, which are the principal export markets for Ghana's wood products, the interventions introduced since 2008 include the following.

- Bilateral agreements between timber-consuming and timber-producing countries to exclude illegal products from trade – most notably the Voluntary Partnership Agreements negotiated under the EU's Action Plan for Forest Law Enforcement, Governance and Trade.
- Broader measures in consumer countries to exclude illegal timber products even in the absence of international agreement. These include the extension of the US Lacey Act to timber, and the EU's 'due diligence' regulation, still under discussion.
- The use of government procurement policy to ensure that only legal (and usually sustainable) timber products are bought by government purchasers.

Ghana has signed the Voluntary Partnership Agreement and exporters are required to be covered by a legal licence, otherwise their products will be refused entry into the EU market. When effectively implemented, these policies will contribute to limiting illegal logging.

Profiles and lines of business of large firms.

John Bitar & Co. Ltd, established in 1955, has grown to become Ghana's leading producer of premium-quality wood products under the Free Zones initiative. Operating three large factories, the company specializes in the manufacture of various products from the finest tropical hardwoods and softwoods. The product range includes sliced veneers, rotary cut veneers, plywood, lumber, mouldings and various profiled sections, laminated and finger-jointed products and flooring. The company is profiled in the next section.

Ayum Forest Products Limited is the second-largest forest reserve concession holder in Ghana and is a subsidiary of the Naja David Group. Recently, the company joined the Global Forest and Trade Network–West Africa (GFTN–West Africa), thereby committing its forest concessions to be responsibly managed, including through the use of credible certification

systems. In addition to the forest concessions under the company's management, it also agreed to implement responsible procurement policies for
the timber entering sawn wood, veneer and plywood mills. The company's
forest reserves are crucial to the conservation and protection of biodiversity
in the Guinean Moist Forest Eco-region, which is considered the most
biodiverse region in West Africa. By joining with other GFTN–West Africa
participants, who collectively manage over 60% of Ghana's productive
forests, Ayum Forest Products stands to have a significant impact in
transforming forestry operations in Ghana.

Naja David Group of Companies Ghana is one of the largest manufacturers
and exporters of wood-based products in the West African subregion. The
company contributes nearly 20% to Ghana's total wood production and
export trade and has over 450 employees.

With substantial investments in plant, resource development, its workforce and to the communities in which it operates, the group is committed
to remaining in the forest and wood products industry. It operates its own
plywood sales and distribution outlet in Kumasi in the Ashanti region. Naja
David Group of Companies Ghana is affiliated to Amerind Pty Limited
in Australia, Amerind Limited in the UK and Timb-Mak Export GmbH in
Germany.

Kpogas Furniture Company Limited is a privately owned Ghanaian limited
liability company incorporated in 1995. The company produces high-
quality furniture products for the local and subregional markets and
employs over 200 people.

Kpogas Furniture Company originally began as a sole-proprietorship
business in 1987 in a suburb of Accra. The company was set up by Reverend
Workannyo Kofi Agbo, who has been the managing director since the
inception of the firm. He is also a minister of the gospel of the Royalhouse
Chapel International.

In 1995 the company was registered as a private limited liability company
with the objective of manufacturing comfortable, high-quality, affordable furniture. The company's head office is now in Odorkor; it has two
showrooms in Accra and one each in Kumasi and Takoradi.

The company manufactures household, office and classroom furniture.
Its office range includes desks, conference tables and chairs. The household
range includes sofas, cabinets and entertainment units, as well as kitchen
cabinets and dining sets. Its bedroom furniture includes beds, dressers and
wardrobes.

Kpogas products sell mainly to middle- and higher-income consumers,
in both the domestic and international markets. The company exports

some of its products to Togo, Ivory Coast and Benin, where the Ghanaian embassies are key clients.

An informal cluster: Kumasi Wood Market. Kumasi is traditionally an important centre for wood products and the Kumasi Wood Market is one of the main wood markets in the country. It began more than 60 years ago in a suburb of Kumasi (Anloga), the second largest city in Ghana, and covered an area of about 15 hectares. The market was run by lumber brokers, who obtained their wood stocks from sawmills and chainsaw operators. The main activities were sales of lumber and secondary and tertiary processing of illegal lumber. Recently, the market was relocated to Sokoban Wood Village, which was jointly funded by the French and Ghanaian governments at a cost of about US$10 million. This ultramodern facility was designed to accommodate almost 1,000 business entities on more than 12 hectares. Relocating the market displaced about 8,000 people engaged in various business ventures; 141 permanent structures were demolished in the first quarter of 2010.

Rationale for selecting profiled firms. John Bitar & Co. Ltd is Ghana's leading producer of premium-quality wood products under the Free Zones initiative.

9.2   Profiles of Major Firms

9.2.1   *John Bitar & Co. Ltd*

Basic details. John Bitar & Co. Ltd is a limited liability company established in 1961 to undertake logging and sawmilling activities and to export high-grade tropical hardwood timber to the European, North American and African markets. A family business, it has its headquarters at Mempeasem, Sekondi and two plants at Sefwi Dwinase near Sefwi Wiawso and at Apowa near Takoradi, all in the Western region of Ghana. The company has a total forest concession of 1,000 km^2 comprising 536 km^2 of forest reserve and 464 km^2 of off reserve.

The company employs over 3,700 workers and has an annual turnover of over US$39 million per annum.

History. The firm was established by John Rachid Bitar, a Ghanaian of Lebanese origin, who had been a cash crop farmer in the Brong Ahafo region.

In 1968, John Bitar & Co. Ltd acquired R. T. Briscoe, a timber-processing company in Sekondi. John Bitar & Co. Ltd moved its operational headquarters to Sekondi in 1999. In that same year, John Bitar & Co. Ltd acquired Gliksten West Africa Limited, a timber-processing company based in Sefwi Wiawso in the Western region.

In 2006, John Bitar & Co. Ltd acquired Metrostar Limited, a plywood processing plant based in Apowa, near Takoradi. In 2010, the company acquired concessions in Gabon.

Current activities and products. John Bitar & Co. Ltd is involved in logging and downstream activities including sawmilling, veneer milling and moulding. The company is also involved in plantation development and reforestation and is currently managing three reforestation projects.

The product lines include kiln-dried and air-dried lumber, sliced veneer, rotary veneer, plywood, dowels, moulding and profiled sections (solid and finger-jointed skirting, picture frames, blanks and component doors, furniture, drawers and joinery), parquet and laminated products.

Organization and management. John Bitar & Co. Ltd has a six-member board with John Bitar as chairman. A seven-member management team includes the managing director, two general managers, an administrative manager, a chief accountant, a production coordinator and a transport engineer.

Firm capabilities. The company has a log input capacity of 200,000 m^3 per annum. Its sawmill has the capacity to process over 18,000 m^3 of lumber, strips, shorts and blanks annually. It produces sliced veneer, rotary veneer, plywood and moulding. John Bitar & Co. Ltd processes over 15 different species of wood.

John Bitar & Co. Ltd's operations are guided by local and international quality control, regulatory and certification requirements. These include the statutory requirements of the Timber Industry Development Division and the Forest Services Commission certification for exports to the UK, the EU and North America. The company has been granted a Controlled Wood Certificate and a Chain of Custody Certificate by the Forest Services Commission.

Given the increasing demand for certified wood products and timber from legally verified sources, the firm is working in partnership with the World Wildlife Fund under its GFTN programme and with the Rainforest Alliance under its SmartWood programme towards achieving Chain-of-Custody certification.

Competition. John Bitar & Co. Ltd's main local competitors include Samantex and Mondial. There is also competition from low-price imports from China and elsewhere.

Supply and marketing chain. All inputs (wood species) are sourced locally from its concession. The main species include wawa, mahogany, edinan, utile, candollei, ekki, chenchen, sapele, odum (iroko), asanfina and ceiba. Newer and lesser-used species such as denya, deltis, yaya and waabima are also being developed.

Only 5% of output is sold on the domestic market. Some 25% is exported within West Africa with most of the remaining 70% going to Europe.

Challenges. John Bitar & Co. Ltd's main concern relates to the destruction of its reserves by illegal chainsaw operators. The influx of low-price imports from China, the high cost of utilities, foreign exchange losses due to the depreciation of the local currency, and fluctuation of prices on the international market are major concerns.

Development agenda. John Bitar & Co. Ltd is aiming to embark on a technology drive with forest research institutions to intensify plantation development of degraded forest (reserves and off reserve), invest in a power-generation system and increase its turnover. The company also aims to expand its operation to Liberia and Gabon.

Chapter 10

BUILDING AND CONSTRUCTION

10.1 Sector Profile

Background and overview. The share of GDP associated with the building and construction sector increased from 4.5% in 1975 to 8.5% in 2000. Over the next few years, the sector continued to grow rapidly, but the annual growth rate slowed from 15% in 2007 to 12% in 2008, and since then the sector has contracted somewhat. The government is the major sponsor of infrastructure projects (building and construction) and dominates the sector.

Structure of the industry. The activities of the major construction companies comprise

- heavy construction, including civil projects such as dams, sewer systems, roads, railways and infrastructure;
- commercial building, including apartments, offices, retail, hotels, schools and public buildings; and
- residential building.

It also includes remodelling, renovating, adding to existing structures and removing them.

Supply and marketing chain. Foreign firms dominate the industry due to their size, capacity and technical expertise, which is well suited to large works such as major road building and infrastructure projects.

Local construction companies are mostly medium or small scale. The majority are family owned and have limited financial resources, and are consequently unable to handle major projects. They are largely involved in the construction of feeder roads, urban roads and small and medium-sized buildings.

Following the enactment of the Public Procurement Act of 2003 (Act 663), all public projects go through a local or international bidding procurement process.

Cement, stones and bitumen are purchased mainly from local sources, while most fittings, furnishings and fixtures are imported from Europe, the US, Dubai and China.

Policy context. The formal segment of the industry is highly regulated. Contractors work with national, regional and district administrative structures to obtain building permits and to have work inspected and certified.

Initiatives are being undertaken by the government to boost the performance of the sector: a building code has been developed, there has been a review of existing housing policy and a better legal and institutional framework has been established. Access to financing remains a major challenge for local construction companies. Most financial institutions lack the funds to provide long-term support. Reliance on short-term funding has been one of the reasons for the relatively high cost of funding projects.

Contractor classification. The Ministry of Roads and Transport categorizes contractors into categories A, B, C and S.[1] The classifications are based on the contractors' technical and managerial expertise, their financial standing, their previous experience, and their plant capacity, equipment and logistics. The criteria for selecting specific contractors are determined by the size and scope of the project.

Challenges. The biggest challenge facing local contractors is their limited capacity (financial, logistical and technical expertise), which excludes them from winning major public infrastructure projects. Most construction projects require contractors to post bid bonds – and the larger the project, the higher the bid bond. Another issue relates to delays by government in paying for services. Other issues include a weak registration regime to classify contractors and weak oversight by government agencies in monitoring and evaluation.

Competitiveness. There is strong competition among the many local companies for small projects, but none of the local companies has the capacity to compete for large projects; projects such as major highways, dams and stadia are almost all undertaken by multinational companies.

Current trends and recent developments. The newly developing oil sector, together with interlinked businesses, is expected to strengthen the size of the construction sector. With a growing population and rising incomes,

---

[1] Category A covers top construction companies (mainly multinationals), while category S covers small construction companies (which are mainly local).

Ghana is facing a sharp rise in demand for private and public housing. According to the Ministry for Water Resources, Works and Housing, Ghana needs to develop 140,000 housing units annually but is only delivering around 40,000. This has led to a housing deficit of approximately one million units. According to the 2011 national budget, a total of 11,199 km of routine maintenance activity and 6,635 km of periodic maintenance activity on the trunk road network needs to be scheduled. Some 201 km of minor rehabilitation work is expected to be undertaken, while major development works for over 200 km of road projects are expected to continue in the 2011 fiscal year.

The residential, retail and office space segments of the construction market have seen significant growth over the past five years. The residential component of the market has been characterized by the development of high-rise projects including the Millennium City project in Accra. There is a strong residential demand for condominiums within the cities and gated communities on the outskirts of major cities. On the commercial side, within the next three years a total of 100,000 m^2 of retail space will be developed in Accra between Independence Avenue and Airport City. In addition, a large number of high-rise office spaces are to be developed, adding about 150,000 m^2 of prime office space.

The government sector, on the other hand, is expected to continue to generate strong demand for major infrastructure and road projects such as dams, interchanges, hospitals, schools, housing and other programmes. Inflows from the oil sector are expected to strengthen the government's budget to fund these programmes.

Profiles and lines of business of large and medium-sized firms. Five leading firms – African Concrete Products, PW Ghana, De Simone, Micheletti & Co. and Metalex Ghana Limited – are profiled fully in the next section. Here, we look at two of the sector's medium-sized firms.

Bessblock Concrete Products Limited, registered in October 1999, is a joint venture between the Social Security and National Insurance Trust (SSNIT), which owns 60% of the company, and Regimanuel Gray Limited, which owns 40%. Its concrete products manufacturing facility was officially commissioned in July 2001.

Bessblock Concrete Products is headquartered at La with two sales outlets, and it has a distribution reach in all ten regions of Ghana. It has a workforce of about 40 (including key management personnel), who assist in the production of about 20,000 6″ blocks per day.

Bessblock Concrete Products commenced business at a time when the construction industry was thriving and demand for high-quality raw materials was rising, with a focus on accuracy of dimensions and strength. The company increasingly focused on quality (uniformity of dimensions and strength). It was to meet these demands that the company entered into its joint venture with SSNIT.

Bessblock Concrete Products produces concrete blocks and paving blocks. These include hollow blocks, solid blocks, hexagonal paving, inter-locking paving and rectangular paving blocks. These come in sizes of 5–8″ for blocks and 60–80 mm for pavement blocks. The production system is highly automated and adheres to international best standards.

One feature of the company is the use of a patented cold mist curing system, which ensures that the concrete achieves maximum strength and is usable within 24 hours of production. The production system is capable of producing uniform and accurate sizes, as well as varying strength levels to meet customer specifications. The concrete blocks are strong enough to be unaffected by handling and transportation. It is one of the few companies that deliver blocks on steel pallets.

The production process involves four main processes; mixing, moulding, curing and cubing. The process begins when river sand, chippings, quarry dust and cement are mixed together with water as a binding agent. The mix is discharged into the filling box as it passes and feeds in its load across the top of the mould. The products are shaped with the help of compaction, and as they leave the press machine they are visually checked before being carried from the block-making machine to the curing chambers. Following a second quality check, the product is stacked for delivery.

Bessblock Concrete Products is now aiming to extend its product lines and is considering acquiring or merging with another similar company.

West Coast Construction Limited, owned by Daniel Opoku, manufactures concrete roof tiles, paving stones, designed concreted slab blocks and quarry aggregates. The company, together with two sister companies (West Coast Quarries and Shai Hills), has an annual turnover of about US$6 million. The company employs over 140 people.

West Coast Construction was established in 1991 by Opoku. The company started out in his residence at East Legon, with an initial workforce of six people. It manufactured concrete products and undertook landscaping, construction and paving works. Prior to the establishment of the company, Opoku operated an electrical shop. He was also a housing contractor.

In 1995, when the workforce reached 60, he moved the office from his residence to a property on Spintex Road that serves as a factory site and head office.

In 1999, Opoku acquired a stone quarry located at Shai Hills in the Greater Accra region from the government and named it West Coast Stone Quarry. The quarry provided aggregates both to the company and to numerous clients. In 2004, the company acquired another quarry, at Yawkwei, near Konogo in the Ashanti region of Ghana, from the government. Each quarry produces over 15 different types of product, including quarry dust, chippings of various sizes, ready-mixed aggregate for concrete use, stone base, highway standard chippings, basic materials, boulders from primary blasts and selected boulders of various sizes. The products from the quarries are mainly sold to road contractors, estate developers or individuals or they are used by the company. West Coast Construction operated these two quarries until 2008, when it leased its quarry at Shai Hills to a Chinese Firm for a period of five years. At this time it was renamed Orient Quarries.

As part of its operations, until 2008 the company manufactured and exported roofing tiles to the subregional markets including Togo, Burkina Faso and Mali. After 2008 the production of roofing tiles by the company was stopped due to a decline in demand for local roofing tiles. The company now imports shingles from the US which it sells on the local market. The main issues that the company faces are the high costs of utilities and building materials, the difficulty in accessing finance and high interest rates. In 2010 the company acquired over 400 hectares of mango and orange plantation.

Small-scale, informal and peripheral activities. Small-scale and informal activities include the following.

Engineering and architectural consultants. There are over 100 private small and medium-sized firms in this category, together employing over 500 consultants.

Construction rental and leasing. Construction rental and leasing is gaining importance as the industry grows.

Small-scale builders. There are many local firms and individuals operating on an informal and unregulated basis.

Sand and stone supply. There are many sand and stone contractors who use their own transport to convey materials to the construction site. Again, they are mostly informal companies.

Water supply. Due to the irregularities in water supply through the national mains, private companies and individuals who own tankers provide water supplies to the sector. Most such arrangements are informal and are largely unregulated.

Rational for selecting profiled firms.   African Concrete Products Limited is the oldest precast concrete manufacturer. PW Ghana is the largest provider of mining support services to mining companies. De Simone Limited and Micheletti & Co. are two of Ghana's top building and civil engineering and construction companies. Metalex Ghana Limited is a leading manufacturer of roofing materials.

10.2   Profiles of Major Firms

10.2.1   African Concrete Products Limited

Basic details.   African Concrete Products (ACP) is a limited liability company established in 1956 to produce precast concrete.

ACP is registered with the Ministry of Water Resources, Works and Housing as a general building contractor and a civil works contractor. Its D1 status enables it to bid for general building works of value over US$500,000, while its category K1 status enables the company to undertake civil works with a contract value up to US$500,000.

ACP has a turnover in excess of US$2 million and a workforce of over 300 employees.

History.   ACP is a private company founded in 1956 by Schoekbeton HBG (a Dutch firm) and A. R. Boakye (a Ghanaian). Prior to establishing the company, Boakye owned Volta Lines, a shipping company. The company is currently owned by Ghanaian private shareholders and by the workers of the company (who hold about 5% of the shares in the company). The company has several satellite production plants, all located in Accra: the roof tile plant, the batching plant, the block making plant, the pipes plant, the kerbs plant and the slabs plant. The company's roof tile plant is the largest plant in Africa and has a capacity of 44,000 tiles per day.

ACP has a wide clientele including government institutions, private institutions, real estate developers, contractors and individuals. Over the past 50 years the company has been able to remain competitive despite challenges in accessing credit, the high cost of utilities and competition from many smaller firms.

Current activities and products.   ACP specializes in the manufacturing of concrete products, constructing prefabricated concrete structures and undertaking building and civil engineering work. The range of products the company produces includes precast septic tanks, building blocks, pipes, roof tiles, paving blocks and other specialized products such as spiral staircases, facing tiles, u-drains, p-trap gulleys, concrete transmission poles, roman balustrades, decorative blocks, concrete fencing posts and coping.

Organization and management.   ACP has a seven-member board and a six-member management team comprising the CEO, a general manager, a production manager, a human resources manager, an accountant and a sales manager.

Firm capabilities.   ACP produces 58 different concrete products, all of which are manufactured to the standards of the British Precast Concrete Federation.

The quality control and research department ensures that both raw materials and finished products meet the requisite industry standards. All raw materials are thoroughly screened and analysed to assess suitability for production. Finished products undergo rigorous quality testing before sale.

Competition.   The company faces competition on two levels. First, Construction Pioneers, Trasacco, Blafla and Micheletti produce similar products to those of ACP. Second, the company faces limited competition from around 100 small unregistered construction firms in Accra that supply lower-quality products at lower prices. Considerable problems surround the enforcement of compliance with standards by the Ghana Standards Board.

Supply and marketing chain.   Sand, cement and aggregate (different grades of stones) are supplied locally. Pigments, used for colouring the roofing tiles produced, are the only imported input and are supplied by a local company that imports from China.

Transportation of finished products is outsourced.

Development agenda.   The key elements in ACP's development agenda are to replace old equipment with new and to expand operations to the subregional market. The company is building a new block factory at its Pokuase site with capacity to produce 50,000 pavement blocks and 28,000 solid blocks a day. The company also aims to influence the imposition and enforcement of products standards in the industry.

10.2.2   PW Ghana Limited

Basic details.   PW Ghana is a member of the PW Group, a leading company in infrastructure development in Africa. PW started its operations in

Ghana in 1995 and it now offers a broad spectrum of civil engineering, contract mining and construction services. Located at East Legon in Accra, PW Ghana has a workforce of 500 full-time personnel (Ghanaians), 20 expatriate personnel and between 100 and 150 contract personnel. The turnover of the company was $30 million in 2010.

History.   The PW Group was founded in Ireland in 1948 as a private civil engineering company and it expanded its operations into Europe over the years. The company made inroads into Africa by starting operations in Nigeria in 1973, and later set up in other African countries. PW Ghana was established in 1994 and began full operations in 1995 as a contract mining company.

Current activities and products.   PW Ghana's activities include earth moving, opencast mining, road and bridge building, construction of industrial and residential buildings and airports, oil and gas services and water supply and sewerage.

The current core business of PW Ghana is the provision of support services to mining companies in Ghana, especially gold mining companies. The company also provides assistance in the area of feasibility studies for mine development and expansion.

Other works include the building of airports, bridges and dams. The company is also involved in the construction of roads and residential buildings.

Organization and management.   The head of PW's operations in Ghana is a general manager who reports directly to the CEO/managing director of the group. The general manager is supported by four functional heads in charge of logistics, maintenance, finance and administration.

Firm capabilities.   The company has the necessary logistics to undertake projects of all sizes. Equipment maintenance is of prime importance due to the challenging locations in which it operates.

Competition.   A current challenge relates to the large number of Chinese contractors who have entered the market, and who compete with the PW Group and other construction companies in the building and civil engineering segments of the industry.

Supply and marketing chain.   Cement, bitumen, electrical goods, plumbing materials, sand and stones are sourced locally, while protective gear and spares for machinery may be imported directly. Items such as plant and geotechnical equipment are also imported.

The company has a quarry that was set up to supply aggregates.

Development agenda. PW Ghana's agenda for the next five years is to expand its business in the development of residential properties. It aims to seek new opportunities and relationships in contract mining for gold mines. It also aims to develop its capacity to provide finance for clients on suitable projects.

10.2.3 De Simone Limited

Basic details. De Simone is one of Ghana's leading building and civil engineering and construction companies. With over 40 years' presence in the country, it is the construction arm and flagship company of the De Simone Group, which comprises seven companies. De Simone is located in the Tema Industrial Area in the Greater Accra region. It employs over 600 personnel, of which 17% are permanent staff. The company's annual turnover was about US$17 million in 2010.

History. De Simone is a private company established in 1964 by Giovanni De Simone, an Italian immigrant. The company, which was originally located in the industrial area in Accra, moved to its current site in Tema in the 1990s.

De Simone started an expansion programme into other West African countries in the 2000s and currently has operations in Burkina Faso (De Simone BF), Nigeria (Monterosa Constructions Ltd) and Liberia (De Simone Liberia Limited).

De Simone is currently headed by Enrico De Simone, a third-generation descendant of the founder.

Current activities and products. The core business of De Simone is civil engineering, mining and residential and commercial construction. The company has built and refurbished several commercial and residential properties in Ghana, including the Accra High Court, Kaneshie Market, Valco Trust House, Tobacco House, Achimota Brewery, Silver Star Towers, Accra Airport, the Ghana Civil Aviation Authority building, the American Embassy and Accra Mall.

De Simone has also undertaken projects in Niger and Mali. In Mali, De Simone was directly involved in the construction of all the infrastructure for Anglo Gold's Yatela Gold Mine project. The company constructed 80 houses, the clubhouse for the expatriate staff village, a 5 km pipeline and all civil works for the plant (primary and secondary crushers, foundations and floor slabs for warehouses, conveyor footings, etc.).

Organization and management.   The De Simone Group comprises nine departments, each headed by a separate manager. De Simone is headed by a managing director, who reports to the group's CEO.

Firm capabilities.   De Simone provides core services in civil engineering, mining and residential and commercial construction and has the capacity to execute large and complex projects. The company has the capacity to execute several projects concurrently, can undertake projects under difficult conditions and has a record of delivering on time. The company also operates in compliance with stringent health and safety standards.

De Simone has a large stock of plant and equipment. In the mining sector, for example, a large fleet of excavators, payloaders and haulers provides coordinated services to excavate, load and haul ore out of mined areas and transport it to the processing area.

The company has a well-equipped workshop, and has engineers trained by the original equipment manufacturers at each site.

Competition.   De Simone's main competitors are Consar Ghana Limited, Taysec Construction Ghana Ltd and Micheletti. In addition to these companies, De Simone faces competition from Chinese construction companies that have entered the industry.

Supply and marketing chain.   De Simone sources sand, concrete, stones, granite chippings (supplied from its sister company, Eastern Quarries) and bitumen locally. Plant and equipment is either directly imported or purchased via companies that import from Germany and Italy.

Exports.   The company has operations and executes projects in Mali, Niger, Nigeria, Burkina Faso and Liberia, with assistance from companies within the parent group.

Challenges.   Competition from Chinese construction companies has increased the intensity of competition that facies the traditional companies in the sector. Despite these challenges, De Simone attracts projects that require quality standards that the Chinese companies operating in Ghana cannot meet at the prices they currently quote.

Development agenda.   De Simone plans to expand its operations into other African countries over the next five years.

10.2.4   Micheletti & Co. Limited

Basic details.   Micheletti & Co. is one of Ghana's leading civil engineering and building construction companies. The company was established by an

Italian entrepreneur, F. Micheletti, and is located in Pantang, a suburb on the outskirts of Accra.

History.   The company was initially registered in 1955 under the name 'F. Micheletti'. In 1963, the name was changed to Micheletti & Co. and the firm was incorporated as a private limited liability company under the Companies Code of 1963 (Act 179).

The company's formation was a direct response to the identification by F. Micheletti of a gap in the market in the construction industry. A contractor by profession, Micheletti immigrated to Ghana in the 1950s and observed that the construction industry was responding poorly to the needs of customers in terms of quality and timely delivery. By focussing on these issues, the company made a mark on the Ghanaian construction industry for almost 22 years under the then managing director, Renato Noce. In 1967, Micheletti sold the company to Noce, who continued to operate under the Micheletti name.

Noce successfully ran the business for another 37 years until, as a result of ill health, he decided to sell the company to two Italian businessmen.

Under these new owners, the company went through a period of restructuring. In 2007, the company won its first large-scale contract: to refurbish the Accra Sports Stadium (Ohene Djan Sports Stadium) in readiness for the 2008 Africa Cup of Nations. The project was delivered on time and within budget – a feat which won the company its reputation for timely quality delivery. In 2009 the company was awarded the contract to refurbish Ghana's national hockey pitch.

Current activities and products.   Micheletti's core business is the engineering, design and construction of civil works (i.e. commercial, sports and residential properties). Under its current ownership, the company is part of a broader group of companies engaged in civil engineering.

Organization and management.   The board of directors includes the two shareholders and the managing director. Two general managers oversee the several departments: auditing, human resources, logistics and procurement, finance and administration, design, yard and commercial.

Firm capabilities.   Micheletti's core competence lies in its capacity to deliver top-quality services on time, avoiding cost escalations that result from delays. The resources available to the company include technical expertise, modern equipment, good logistics and access to finance. The company offers planning, design, feasibility studies, technical, logistical, legal, environmental, financial and impact analyses, and a comprehensive range of other services throughout the life cycle of a project.

Competition. The construction industry is very competitive and the government's liberalization policy has contributed to an influx of foreign construction companies into Ghana. As one of Ghana's largest construction companies, Micheletti's main direct local competitors are De Simone Ghana Limited, Consar Construction Limited and Taysec Construction Limited. Other competitors include Regimanuel Gray Construction Ltd and Trasacco Estates Development Company.

The biggest challenge for Micheletti is the arrival of Chinese construction firms. Most of the contracts awarded to these firms are tied directly to loan facilities from the Chinese government and financial institutions in China. Most government projects financed by the Chinese government and by Chinese banks are automatically awarded to Chinese construction companies without a procurement process that would allow local companies to submit bids.

The key to competitive survival for Micheletti lies in the quality of service it delivers and its timely delivery, which most competitors currently find very difficult to match.

Supply and marketing chain. Once a tender/bid is won, a team meeting is held to agree a timescale and tasks are assigned. Once the project is underway, the process is tightly controlled to avoid delays. The company imports most of its building materials from Italy to maintain quality assurance.

Development agenda. Micheletti aims to move into more intensive use of prefabricated materials. This will reduce the price of inputs and the cost of procurement.

10.2.5 Metalex Ghana Limited

Basic details. Metalex is a family business established in 1984 to produce competitively priced high-quality roofing materials. Situated in a suburb of Accra, the company started as a retailer of aluminium roofing sheets but later became a manufacturer of aluminium, clay and plastic roofing materials. The company has other factories producing clay roofing products and plastic roofing products.

History. Metalex is a private family business owned by Kwabena Adjare Danquah, a Ghanaian businessman. The history of the company dates back to 1980 when, upon completion of high school, Danquah joined his father's retail business. In 1981, with a loan of US$5,000 from his father, he started a small business selling steel filing cabinets. In 1983, Danquah became a salesman and stockist for Ghana Aluminium Products, the largest manufacturer of roofing materials in Ghana. Through his retail business he built up a good understanding of the industry and, in 1984, he decided to move into manufacturing by establishing Metalex to produce roofing sheets.

Danquah travelled to the UK to seek equipment to manufacture aluminium roofing sheets. Realizing that the equipment could be produced much more cheaply in Africa, he sought the assistance of a South African engineer, who eventually manufactured the necessary equipment for him. This completed the firm's transition into manufacturing.

Current activities and products. The core business of Metalex is the manufacture of metal and brick roofing materials. Clay products include building, roofing and flooring products. Metal products include roofing sheets and screws. The roofing sheets also come in aluminium, galvanized steel and stone-coated duratil. Plastic products include tongue and groove (T&G) roofs and accessories.

The company also imports roofing sheets from South Africa.

The company undertakes several secondary activities, including real estate development. As a group of companies, Metalex also has an investment in a radio station.

Organization and management. Metalex has a workforce of about 300 people. The founder of the company, Kwabena Danquah, is the CEO of the company, while his son Yaw Danquah is the general manager. The general manager oversees five line managers who control human resources, sales, marketing, production and security. It is noteworthy that Metalex believes in keeping security in-house rather than outsourcing it: this is to enable the company to ensure full internal and external controls. The next level consists of junior staff, some of whom are trainees while others are on the production floor.

Firm capabilities. The core capability of Metalex lies in its ability to produce and sell at prices below that of its competitors. The flexibility of the production process allows the company to satisfy a wide range of customers. Diversification also contributes to the success of the company. Metalex also owns a clay brick facility that allows it to offer alternative solutions for customers. Together with its plastic roofing manufacturing facility, Metalex is the only roofing company in Ghana that covers aluminium sheet, clay and plastic products.

The company has also mastered the just-in-time production process, which allows it to turn orders around faster than any of its competitors.

In addition to the above, Metalex has modern plant and equipment as well as the requisite human capital with the required technical expertise. This has been bolstered by a continuous training and capacity development programme that is offered to the staff. This allows the company to innovate and regularly introduce new products onto the market. As a result of its innovative products and market leadership, the company has won several awards from the Ghana Real Estate Developers Association for its pioneering designs of roofing sheets.

Competition.   In the aluminium and steel roofing segment, Metalex faces competition from Aluworks, Domod Aluminium, Trouselina, Raincoat Roofing System and Rockster. Metalex enjoys strong relationships with suppliers and financiers that allow it to buy raw materials in bulk at preferential prices and with discounts. Metalex sells to some of its competitors, such as Trouselina, because of the price advantages it enjoys from suppliers.

In the plastic T&G segment, Metalex's main competitor is Interplast.

Imports from China continue to be a major competition challenge.

Metalex operates the just-in-time production process. The company offers innovative services such as free quantity surveying, site measurement, installation recommendations and a roofing helpline.

Supply and marketing chain.   Steel coils and frames are imported from South Africa. The prices of imports are of crucial importance to the company, and Metalex initially entered into a joint venture with Macsteel, a South African company, which manufactured and supplied steel coils. Under the contract, Metalex was forced to buy the products irrespective of price. When the relationship with Macsteel collapsed in 2004, Danquah entered into a 50:50 joint venture with Comet Steel of South Africa to establish Macsteel Ghana. Under this arrangement, Comet Steel produces steel coils that Metalex is free to buy if prices are competitive. This gave Metalex improved access to steel coils at competitive prices.

After-sales support is provided through a sales helpline. Metalex has a network of independent installers who are trained by the company. They operate in all areas of the country.

Exports.   The company currently exports products to West African countries including Nigeria, Burkina Faso, Mali and Togo.

Development agenda.   Within five years, Metalex will expand its operations into warehousing across the country. Metalex plans to establish a facility in Liberia and expand supply to other countries in West Africa. In the long term, the company will also consider investment in mining to enable them to have direct access to raw materials for aluminium production.

Chapter 11

CEMENT AND QUARRYING

11.1 Sector Profile

Background and overview. The rapid growth of the construction sector has led to increasing demand for cement over the past decade. The contribution of the construction sector to GDP rose from US$1.1 billion in 2006 to US$2.5 billion in 2010. Demand for Portland cement was estimated to be about 4.5 million mt in 2009.[1] Demand increased to 4.8 million mt in 2010 and is forecast to rise further to 5.5 million mt in 2012. This represents an annual growth rate of 7.0% (Table 11.1).

Structure of the cement industry. Prior to the market liberalization of 2000, the cement industry was a monopoly, with Ghana Cement Works Limited (GHACEM) as the only domestic producer.

There are now three domestic producers. Two are based in the south of the country: GHACEM has two plants, at Tema and Takoradi, with a total production capacity of about 2.4 million mt; and Diamond Cement has a grinding mill located in the Volta region with a capacity of 1.2 million mt. Savanna Cement Ghana Limited, a fully integrated plant with a plant capacity of 300,000 mt, is located in the Northern region. Its clinker production unit is expected to begin operating by March 2012 (Table 11.2).

Total cement output from GHACEM and Diamond Cement Ghana Limited increased from 2.4 million mt in 2003 to 3.9 million mt in 2007.[2]

A large number of small firms, cement distributors and individuals are engaged in the import of bagged cement into Ghana. There are also a few small to medium-sized companies, including Greenview International Co. Ltd (a subsidiary of the Dangote group), that are involved in the import of bulk cement for rebagging and distribution in Ghana (Table 11.3).

Supply and marketing chain. Clinker and gypsum are imported, while limestone is sourced locally. GHACEM uses about 24% local limestone as

---

[1] Ministry of Water Resources, Works and Housing.
[2] Ghana Statistical Service.

TABLE 11.1. Cement demand forecast.

Year	Total demand volume (mt)
2005	3,460,830
2006	3,703,089
2007	3,962,308
2008	4,239,666
2009	4,536,442
2010	4,883,994
2011	5,193,773
2012	5,557,335

Source: Ministry of Water Resources, Works and Housing.

TABLE 11.2. A listing of Ghana's quarries (March 2010).

Region	Number of quarries
Greater Accra	58
Western	79
Eastern	60
Central	45
Volta	14
Ashanti	38
Brong Ahafo	5
Upper East	5
Total	304

Source: Minerals Commission/Sync Consult (2010).

filler, following ISO specifications for the production of cement.[3] Diamond Cement imports clinker and gypsum from Spain and China.

GHACEM has 10 outlets and depots spread across the country. Some wholesalers and retailers buy cement directly from the factories. Transportation is mainly by road.[4] Prices in other regions are higher than in Accra, reflecting transport costs.

Large-scale users buy in bulk direct from the factories. These include mining companies, construction firms, block makers and estate developers. This segment accounts for 15% of output.

Policy context. The government has supported the harnessing of limestone deposits in Buipe, Nauli and Nadowli in the Northern region and

[3] Source: Graham Bell, GHACEM Takoradi Plant works manager.
[4] Bulk cement orders from the mines in the Western region are mainly transported by rail.

TABLE 11.3. Import volumes of cement products.

Year	Import value in GH¢	Import value in US$
2005	128,444,521	142,716,134
2006	152,002,342	167,035,541
2007	191,730,066	206,161,361
2008	258,017,729	245,731,170
2009	236,617,013	169,012,152
2010	299,736,171	209,605,714

Source: Ghana Statistical Service (2010).

other deposits in the Eastern and Western regions for cement production, as well as clay deposits in the Central region that are used in the production of bricks, tiles and ceramics. Through the Ghana Standards Board it has instituted measures to protect buyers from substandard products. Pre-market and post-market control systems are in place, though improvements in enforcement of compliance are needed.

Challenges. The main issues facing the industry are high utility tariffs, especially for electricity, power outages and the high cost of fuel.

Competitiveness. The market remains dominated by GHACEM, though with the entry of new factories there has been increased price competition. The high local production costs mean that cement from Ghana is not competitive in terms of price compared with other West African countries, but the quality of Ghanaian cement is relatively good.

Export status, strength and potential. Ghana exported 1,813 mt of cement to the subregional market in 2007. Exports increased to 47,412 mt in 2008 and to 53,358 mt in 2009 but fell to 25,443 mt in 2010 as more cement was absorbed by the growing domestic market.[5]

Recent developments. Demand for cement in Ghana has been outrunning supply. One producer is now aiming to increase its production capacity by 1 million mt per annum through the installation of additional plant and the upgrading of its packing facility. A new company has recently acquired land in the Western region of Ghana to establish a 1 million mt cement plant.

Rationale for selecting profiled firms. All three cement producers are profiled.

[5] Ghana Export Promotion Council.

11.2   Profiles of Major Firms

11.2.1   GHACEM Limited

Basic details.   GHACEM was founded by the government of Ghana in collaboration with Norcem AS of Norway in 1967 to produce cement for major infrastructure projects in Ghana, especially the Tema motorway, the Akosombo dam and Tema harbour. The company is currently the largest manufacturer of cement in Ghana, with a staff strength of 268. The turnover of the company in 2010 was US$500 million.

History.   In the early 1960s, a Ghanaian entrepreneur, Dr Addison, introduced the government to a Norwegian cement manufacturer, Norcem AS, with a view to setting up a small mill to produce cement for the construction of the Tema motorway, the Akosombo dam and Tema harbour. The plant was eventually set up in 1967 and the capacity of the plant has been increased over time to its present level of 2.4 million mt per annum.

The ownership of the company has changed over the years. The original ownership structure of GHACEM was 75% government of Ghana, 24.5% Norcem AS and 0.5% Dr Addison. In 1993, the government sold 35% of GHACEM's shares to Scancem (formerly Norcem AS), which increased its share to 59.5%, leaving the government with 40% and Dr Addison with 0.5%. In 1997, the Ghana government sold a further 5% of the company (an eighth of its remaining 40% shareholding) to the workers of the company and, in 1999, the government sold the rest of its shares to Scancem. Scancem currently owns 93.1% of the shares in the company, the workers own 5% and the remaining 1.9% is owned by Dr Addison.

In 1999, the Heidelberg Cement Group in Germany took over Scancem. GHACEM is therefore now a subsidiary of the Heidelberg Cement Group.

GHACEM has produced over 30 million mt of cement since its foundation.

Current activities and products.   The company produces two main types of cement, both of which are supplied in bulk and in bags. The first, Super Rapid, has an early setting time of between 2 and 7 days. The second, Ghacem Extra, has a longer setting time of 28 days.

Organization and management.   GHACEM has a five-member board of directors with a chief operating officer who doubles as the chairman of the board and reports to Heidelberg Cement Africa (HC Africa). The managing director of the company reports to the board and oversees the daily

operations of the company. Reporting to the managing director are functional heads of human resources, finance, corporate affairs, production,
maintenance and shipping and logistics.

Firm capabilities. The production process combines German and Norwegian technology.

The company has two factories – one in Tema and the other in Takoradi, in the Western region of Ghana – each of which has a capacity of
1.2 million mt per annum, bringing current total capacity to 2.4 million mt
per annum. The company is undertaking an expansion project that will
increase the capacity of the plant in Tema to 2.2 million mt per annum
from 2012.

Competition. GHACEM was for 33 years the only manufacturer of cement
in Ghana. In 2000, a second manufacturer, Diamond Cement, entered the
industry. There are currently two further competitors in the industry. The
first, Dangote Cement Ghana Limited, imports bulk cement into Ghana for
rebagging under the name Greenview. The second, Fortress Cement Ghana,
has just entered the market and will produce cement locally.

Supply and marketing chain. GHACEM's main raw materials (clinker,
gypsum and limestone) were all imported until 2004, when the company
invested in a limestone quarry at Yongwase (Krobo) in the Eastern region
to supply limestone. The remaining 75% of its raw material needs (clinker
and gypsum) are still imported.

The group has a trading unit that manages international sourcing.

GHACEM has 10 depots around the country supplying directly to distributors and does not deal directly with the retail market. The company
does, however, sell bulk cement directly to large construction companies
and contractors such as Consar, Taysec, Micheletti, PW Ghana and ACP.

Exports. GHACEM does not currently export any of its products.

Challenges. Prior to 2002, the raw material imports of GHACEM – clinker,
gypsum and limestone – attracted zero rates of tax. However, since 2002
the government has imposed a 5% tax on imports of raw materials by
GHACEM. However, imported cement from other countries in the West
African subregion attracts a zero rate of tax under the ECOWAS protocol,
which gives imported cement products an advantage.

Recent developments. The company plans to expand its annual capacity
by 1 million mt from 2012 onwards in response to a strong growth in
demand.

11.2.2   Eastern Quarries Limited

Basic details.   Eastern Quarries is one of the largest quarries in Ghana in terms of concession size and production volumes – it has an estimated resource life of over 150 years. The company is the market leader for precast and quarry aggregates. The quarry is located at Shai Hills, about 40 km from Accra, and the headquarters of the company is in the Tema Industrial Area. The average turnover of the company is in excess of US$3.3 million per year and it has 150 employees.

History.   Eastern Quarries was founded by a Ghanaian entrepreneur. The company was then acquired by GHACEM to provide stone and aggregates. In 1997, the De Simone Group, a civil engineering and construction group, acquired the quarry from GHACEM and renamed it Eastern Quarries Limited. The company is presently 80% owned by De Simone and 20% owned by Valtiero Bovelacci, who is the managing director. (For a profile of De Simone, see below.)

Current activities and products.   Eastern Quarries produces two broad categories of products: precast products and quarry aggregates. Precast products include pavement blocks, building blocks of sandcrete, concrete and rock mixes, road kerbs for domestic and industrial use and concrete pipes and culverts with C25 strength and above.

The company has an annual capacity of over 2 million mt of quarry aggregates, including quarry dust, surface dressing chippings, asphaltic chippings and sea defence boulders.

Organization and management.   Eastern Quarries has been structured as one of the nine departments of De Simone, its parent company.

Firm capabilities.   The company has three modern crushing plants and operates 10-hour shifts. This enables the company to meet the aggregates needs of De Simone Group as well as those of other clients. The average production capacity of each plant is estimated at 750,000 mt per year. Eastern Quarries produces customized preformed concrete pipes and curb structures, cement building blocks and paving blocks.

All products meet both local (Ghana Standards Board and Ghana Highway Authority) and international standards.

Competition.   The main competitors of Eastern Quarries are ACP Concrete Products Limited, Bafla Concrete Products and Bessblock Concrete Products.

Supply and marketing chain.   With the exception of imported consumables such as spare parts, all raw materials including cement, fuel and lubrication oils are procured locally.

The quarry supplies the companies in the De Simone Group with granite chippings, road bases, concrete structures and cement blocks. The company operates a fleet of vehicles for delivery to companies in the group.

Eastern Quarries also supplies various aggregates to other construction companies and individuals for residential, industrial and infrastructural development across a large area of the Greater Accra region. It has sales offices in Accra and Tema.

Eastern Quarries currently has about 50% of the market share for quarry products in southern Ghana.

Exports.   Eastern Quarries does not export.

Development agenda.   Eastern Quarries aims to diversify its product line by producing roofing tiles and prestressed flat floors. The company will, in the near future, replace its plant and equipment with modern crushing technology to improve efficiency and quality. The company aims to expand its market coverage to neighbouring countries in the West African subregion.

11.2.3   Prime Stone Quarries

Basic details.   Prime Stone Quarries is a privately owned company established in 2008. Located at Apemenyim near Shama Junction, off the Shama–Takoradi road in the Western region, the company produces stone aggregates and related products for the construction industry.

Prime Stone Quarries employs about 100 people and has a turnover of over US$1.5 million per annum.

History.   Prime Stone Quarries is a subsidiary of Veritas Investment Limited, a privately owned Ghanaian company with business interests in surface mining and construction. The company owns a 20-hectare stone quarry located at Apemenyim in the Western region that has a granite reserve of 6 million cubic metres.

When Prime Stone was established in 2008, it acquired Samuel Mensah Stone Quarry and its concessions as well as a number of small-scale stone quarry concessions in Apemenyim. Samuel Mensah Stone Quarry was founded by Samuel Mensah, a Ghanaian entrepreneur. Prior to founding his own company, Mensah was for 10 years involved in the quarry business as a supplier of aggregates, a marketer of quarry products to construction companies and also undertook other activities related to the supply of quarry products.

Current activities and products.   Prime Stone Quarries produces and supplies a wide range of aggregates and grades of stones for road construction, building and civil engineering works. The company produces eight main products: 10 mm aggregate, 14 mm aggregate, 20 mm aggregate, 25 mm aggregate, 30 mm aggregate, rough dust, smooth dust, 0.40 mm chippings and 0.250 mm chippings.

   In addition to these special aggregates products, the company also produces custom products such as sea defence boulders, riprap and railway ballast.

Organization and management.   Prime Stone Quarries has a seven-member board which includes the chairman, the managing director, the executive director, finance consultants and a lawyer. It also has a five-member management team.

Firm capabilities.   Prime Stone Quarries produces eight types of stone aggregates using top-of-the-range Metso equipment and technology. The equipment includes a jaw crusher that can crush about 1000 m^3 of rock over an eight-hour shift running a two-shift system. The company has the capacity to produce all the specifications that are required by companies in the construction sector.

Competition.   The closest local competitors of Prime Stone Quarries in the Western region are West Rock Stone Quarry and Just Mac. In the Central region it competes with Sarcon Quarry Limited and the Great Kosa Stone Quarry.

Supply and marketing chain.   The company's main inputs are wear liners and mantles, ammonia and explosives. The explosives-related inputs include cortex, bulk emulsion boosters, blasting caps, unidet, fuses and snapline. These are sourced from local importers such as Wileb Mining Services and Maxam Ghana Limited.

   These inputs are used to blast rock *in situ* into pieces that are fed into the jaw crusher. A cone crusher breaks the aggregates down further before the result is conveyed to the screen, which sorts the products into various grades and aggregates.

   Finished products are usually transported by a fleet of vehicles belonging to Prime Stone Quarries. In some instances, the aggregates are transported by third parties or by the customers' own trucks.

Exports.   The company does not export.

Challenges.   One problem that Prime Stone Quarries currently faces is a difficulty in establishing compensation levels for farmers currently working on the company's concession. A second of area of concern relates to the local availability of spare parts for equipment. Vendors of spare parts do not stock the parts in the country and therefore they are not readily available when the need arises.

Development agenda.   The company aims to expand its operation through the acquisition of a tertiary crusher to augment current production capacity.

Chapter 12

METALS, ENGINEERING AND ASSEMBLY

12.1   Sector Profile

Background and overview.   The metals, engineering and assembly sector comprises three distinct groups of firms.

The aluminium sector.   Mining of bauxite, production of aluminium and aluminium products.

Iron and steel.   The manufacture of primary iron and steel products from locally sourced scrap, and the production of steel products.

Fabricated metal products.   This covers products such as tanks and reservoirs, structural metal products such as metal doors and screens, window frames and architectural metal work.

Aluminium.   Ghana has large deposits of bauxite, the main raw material for the aluminium industry. Ghana's bauxite deposits, located in Awaso in the Western region, are mined by Ghana Bauxite Company, which has been in operation since 1941. The company produced 420,000 mt of bauxite in 2009 – a smaller amount than the 1 million mt that it produced in 2007 because of operational problems. In 2009, Bonsai, a Chinese mining company, acquired an 80% share in the company, with a view to establishing an alumina refinery with an annual capacity of 1 million mt. There are also deposits of bauxite at Nyinahin in the Ashanti region (estimated deposit: 280 million mt), Kibi in the Eastern region (estimated deposit: 120 million mt) and Mount Ejuanema, also in the Eastern region (estimated deposit: 5 million mt).

Ghana's bauxite is exported to Jamaica for processing into alumina (Al_2O_3) and then reimported into the country to supply the Volta Aluminum Company (VALCO).

VALCO was established in 1960 and is Africa's largest aluminium smelter, processing alumina into primary aluminium ingots ready for fabrication. It relies on the Volta River Authority hydroelectric station at Akosombo to provide its energy needs, consuming 10% of the total power generated by the station when the smelter is operating at full capacity.

The main client of VALCO is Aluworks, a rolling mill which manufactures aluminium products from aluminium ingots or molten alumina. The company is the main source of supply to the downstream aluminium sector, which comprises 15–20 medium-sized companies that manufacture roofing sheets and about 150 small enterprises that produce a wide range of kitchen utensils.

Iron and steel. There are currently four manufacturers of rebar from scrap: Tema Steel Company Limited (which is profiled below), Ferro Fabrik, Special Steel and Western Steel and Forging. Western Steel and Forging also produces nuts and bolts. These four companies combined employ about 2,800 people.

There are three producers of drawn wire products, including Wire Weaving Industries Limited, which is profiled in the next section. It is notable that no company is involved in wire drawing or in galvanizing (steel output volumes in Ghana do not justify the setting up of a galvanizing operation). All these companies import ready-coated wire as their raw material.

United Steel makes hollow squares and round pipes from imported steel sheet sourced from the Ukraine, Russia and China.

A few small firms make nails from imported drawn wire.

Metal fabrication. The leading company in this subsector is Ghana Metal Fabrication Limited, which manufactures a wide range of products. The company is profiled below.

Many small informal enterprises are involved in metal fabrication. The biggest concentration of informal metal fabricators is the Suame Magazine Industrial Development Organization in Kumasi, in the Ashanti region.

Established in 1935, the Suame Magazine is the largest artisan engineering cluster in sub-Saharan Africa. Located about 10 km from Kumasi, the capital of the Ashanti region, it occupies an area of 20 square miles.

The cluster currently contains more than 200,000 fabricators, about 50% of which are engineering enterprises that are involved in the manufacture of metal products and in vehicle repair.[1] The Suame Magazine is noted for having some of the most mature micro- and small-scale metal fabrication enterprises in Africa.[2]

---

[1] McCormick, D. 1998. Enterprise clusters in Africa: on the way to industrialization? Discussion Paper 366, Institute for Development Studies, University of Nairobi, Kenya.

[2] Adeya, N. 2006. *Knowledge, Technology and Growth: The Case Study of Suame Manufacturing Enterprise Cluster in Ghana.* Knowledge for Development (part of the World Bank Institute).

The Suame Magazine serves individuals and private and public corporate bodies from all over the country. It also serves customers from neighbouring West African countries, especially Burkina Faso, Nigeria, Togo, Mali and Ivory Coast.

Dawson categorized the individuals involved into three groups: blacksmiths who used clay and brick forges and hand tools, a middle group that had achieved a modest level of technological enhancement, mostly through the use of locally made machines, and a group that used machine tools, including at least one lathe, that Dawson calls 'engineering workshops'.[3]

While some workers are apprenticed to small enterprises and are not highly skilled, a second group have higher-level technical skills gained during apprenticeships at large enterprises and in technical training institutes. It is the presence of the latter that has led to the cluster producing some items that can compete favourably with imports. Suame's vehicle mechanics manage to achieve greater efficiency than many small-enterprise clusters because they subcontract a great deal of the work to each other in the cluster, enabling the group to achieve economies of scale.

Initiatives have been introduced to support technology development and transfer to enterprises in the cluster. The Technology Consultancy Centre of KNUST in Kumasi was established to act as an interface between researchers at KNUST and the business community. Additionally, the Intermediate Technology Transfer Unit was established in Suame Magazine to develop the capacity of enterprises to design, manufacture and service equipment for agricultural and engineering development. Among the impacts of this intervention is the growth of small foundry businesses in other parts of Ghana. The GRATIS Foundation coordinates a network of Intermediate Technology Transfer Units. The foundation, which was established in 1987 to promote grassroots industrialization and to spread appropriate technology, has helped artisans from Suame to acquire machine tools and equipment for specialized engineering operations.

Given the concentration of basic engineering skills, technical skills and knowhow in the Suame Magazine cluster, the provision of technical assistance in advanced fabrication technologies and information and communication technology could transform the cluster into a substantial contributor to industrialization in Ghana.

[3] Dawson, J. 1988. Small scale industry in Ghana: a case of Kumasi. Report presented to the Economic and Social Committee on Overseas Research (ESCOR)/Overseas Development Administration (ODA), London.

Other companies. Nexans Kabelmetal (Ghana) Limited, which is profiled below, is a subsidiary of Nexans Kabelmetal, a Germany-based
multinational specialist in cables and cabling systems.

The Ghana Cylinder Manufacturing Company Limited (GCMC) is a
state-owned institution, established in 1998, to promote the domestic
use of liquefied petroleum gas. The company has an annual turnover of
US$1.8 million and employs 20 people.

GCMC was originally established to produce only liquefied petroleum
gas cylinders; gas stoves and metal chairs were added to its product lines
later. The company also imports finished stoves and regulators from China,
and these are marketed under the GCMC brand.

The company has an installed capacity to produce 1,050 cylinders
per day. The company is presently operating at 40% of capacity.

The company imports special steel for cylinders from China. Paints,
powder and valves are imported from India. Labels and polythene for the
packaging of the cylinders are acquired locally. GCMC has distributors in
the Ashanti, Eastern, Volta and Greater Accra regions.

The company initially exported to Burkina Faso, Benin, Ivory Coast and
Togo but it now produces only for the domestic market.

Supply chain. Most of the equipment, parts and accessories that are used
by Aluworks and downstream companies are imported. Colour coatings
are available locally from the local paint companies. Some companies rely
on imported coatings for the production of coloured roofing sheets.

Companies in the iron and steel and metal fabrication sectors rely on
the four steel plants. However, as local demand far exceeds the combined
capacities of the domestic plants, most users rely on imported steel from
countries such as the Ukraine, China and India. Imports account for about
50% of local steel demand.

Most of the intermediate and finished products are consumed locally.
Aluworks exports about 45% of its products to Nigeria, the US, the
Caribbean and Europe.

Policy context. The main challenge facing the aluminium industry is the
influx of cheap Chinese aluminium products onto the market. Even though
imported aluminium products attract import duties of up to 40%, they still
sell at lower prices than products produced by Aluworks.

Despite a ban being imposed on the exportation of scrap in 2007, ferrous
scrap continues to be exported, depriving the four steel companies of raw
materials. Most are therefore operating below capacity. This is a major
policy concern.

The cost of electricity is relatively high, and this increases the unit cost of locally manufactured steel and aluminium products.

A recent problem arising from the shutdown of VALCO is that aluminium ingots are now imported from Jamaica, further raising costs.

Export status, strength and potential. Most of the companies in this industry export to countries in the subregion. Tema Steel Company Limited, for example, exports steel to Burkina Faso and Mali. Aluworks, the only rolling mill in West Africa, exports about 45% of its finished products to countries in the West African subregion, especially Nigeria, as well as to Europe, the US and the Caribbean.

Recent developments. The government has long been interested in establishing an integrated alumina industry. The most recent development is the investment by Bonsai, a Chinese mining company (through an 80% shareholding in Ghana Bauxite Company), in the establishment of a 1 million mt per annum alumina refinery.

Rationale for selecting profiled firms. VALCO is the only aluminium smelter in Ghana and Aluworks is the only rolling mill and producer of aluminium ingots in West Africa. Tema Steel Company Limited has been in existence for almost 40 years and is the largest manufacturer of steel products in Ghana. Ghana Metals Company is the largest company in the metals fabrication industry. Nexans Kabelmetal is a global expert in cables and cabling systems. Wire Weaving Industries Limited is Ghana's largest manufacturer of drawn wire and related products.

12.2 Profiles of Major Firms

12.2.1 *Volta Aluminum Company (VALCO)*

Basic details. VALCO is an aluminium smelter that was established in 1960 to exploit Ghana's bauxite deposits and spearhead the development of an integrated aluminium industry. VALCO is currently owned 100% by the government of Ghana. It employs 557 people and has an annual turnover of about US$88 million.

History. VALCO was established under the government of the first president of the Republic of Ghana, Dr Kwame Nkrumah, in partnership with the late Edgar Kaiser, chairman and founder of the Kaiser Aluminum & Chemical Corporation (KACC), which became the original majority shareholder of the company.

Construction of the VALCO plant began in 1964 and commercial production of aluminium began in 1967. Prior to the establishment of VALCO, an agreement was signed between the government of Ghana and KACC for the construction of the Akosombo hydroelectric dam, which was to supply power to VALCO. The Akosombo hydroelectric plant was then 90% owned by KACC and 10% owned by the Reynolds Metal Company, which later became the Aluminum Company of America.

In March 1967, when VALCO produced its first metal for commercial purposes, the plant had a capacity of three cell lines made up of 100 cells per line. Subsequently, the facility was expanded with the construction of the fourth and fifth cell lines in 1970 and 1974, respectively, bringing the total installed capacity to 200,000 mt per year.

VALCO operates five potlines each with an annual production capacity of approximately 40,000 mt of aluminium. However, due to the inability of the Volta River Authority to meet the energy requirements of VALCO, the smelter was shutting down intermittently, and was closed altogether for two years before reopening in 2011.

VALCO has operated at 20% of full capacity since its reactivation in 2011 – it currently produces 3,000 mt of foundry ingots per month for the local and international markets. Half of that production is supplied to Aluworks (profiled below) and Western Rod and Wire Company Limited, another local company that uses foundry ingots and molten aluminium for the production of rods for high-tension cables. VALCO has signed offtake agreements with Aluworks and Western Rod and Wire to purchase 1,500 mt of ingots between them (1,000 mt to Aluworks and 500 mt to Western Rod and Wire); the remaining 1,500 mt of ingots is exported to Europe.

Current activities and products. VALCO smelts alumina to produce aluminium ingots. Its main products are

- low profile sows,
- hot molten metal (supplied to Aluworks),
- extrusion billets (for the manufacture of doors and window frames),
- 22 kg foundry ingots,
- T-ingots,
- rolling slabs,
- processed/unprocessed ingots and
- scrap material.

Organization and management. VALCO has a nine-member board of directors with a management team headed by the chief executive officer, four deputy chief executive officers and four functional heads.

Competition. As Ghana's only aluminium smelter, VALCO currently enjoys a local monopoly in the production and supply of aluminium ingots and molten alumina.

Supply and marketing chain. VALCO's main raw materials are alumina, petroleum coke and power. Alumina is imported from China and the US. Even though Ghana has abundant deposits of bauxite from which alumina can be produced, there are no local supplies of alumina due to the absence of a bauxite mill in the country. The company imports petroleum coke from a number of countries in Europe as well as from China. Electricity is supplied locally by GRIDCo Limited (the distributor for the Volta River Authority). The company sells directly to local companies such as Aluworks in Accra and Western Rods in the Western region of Ghana.

Exports. VALCO exports its products to Aluminum Company of America Europe and to the ECOWAS region.

Challenges. VALCO's main issue is the availability of energy to fully power all the potlines of its smelter. In addition, the high unit cost of power can undermine the competitiveness of the smelter.

Recent developments. The company's current restructuring, which is the result of a change in ownership, has impacted positively on its operations. As part of the restructuring, capital injection has enabled the company to acquire new technology and machinery to boost its production cycle and levels.

Development agenda. VALCO aims to increase its production levels to full capacity.

12.2.2 Aluworks Limited

Basic details. Aluworks is an ISO certified aluminium manufacturing company and is the only rolling mill in West Africa. The company produces sheet metal either for onward supply to tertiary manufacturers of construction materials (such as Metalex, Domod and Pioneer Aluminium Factory and Ghana Aluminium Company) or for production of materials for the construction and housing industry (e.g. roofing sheets, water tanks and louvre blades), the household industry (e.g. hollowware and basins) and the transport industry.

The company is currently listed on the Ghana Stock Exchange.

History. Aluworks was incorporated as a private limited liability company on 22 March 1978 as part of the government of Ghana's integrated aluminium project. The construction of the factory commenced in 1982 and the factory was completed and officially commissioned in 1985. The company was set up with an initial production capacity of 30,000 mt per annum.

The company was originally owned by Kaiser Aluminum Plant, a US company that has been in Ghana since 1965, and VALCO (also known as Kaiser US). Aluminium ingots, the main input of the rolling process, are produced from bauxite.

Aluworks enjoyed a monopoly position in the industry as the only manufacturer of sheet metal for roofing sheets, louvre blades, etc., which are the intermediate products for companies that manufacture construction materials. In 1996, as a result of an economic recession as well as several difficulties encountered by VALCO, its main supplier, Aluworks went through a difficult phase. The company faced stiff competition from an influx of cheaper intermediate products from China.

On 29 November 1996, Aluworks became a public limited liability company and listed on the Ghana Stock Exchange. Under the public listing, the government of Ghana sold its shares under an Initial Public Offering. The major shareholders – the Ghana Cocoa Board, the Social Security and National Insurance Trust (SSNIT) and Strategic Initiatives Limited – hold 75% of the company's shares between them. The rest of the shares are held by other companies and by individual Ghanaian citizens.

The change in shareholding came with a change in focus from a process-driven approach to a more marketing-driven one, which helped to reposition the company in the market.

In 2002 VALCO faced several challenges arising from negotiations with the Electricity Company of Ghana, its sole provider of power. This led to the government shutting down the operations of VALCO in May 2003.

Following Aluworks's strategic shift in direction and the subsequent reopening of VALCO in 2006, Aluworks started to recover, eventually posting a positive net profit in 2010.

Current activities and products. As the only rolling mill in Ghana, Aluworks has enjoyed a monopoly position since 1978.

The company's current production level is 20,000 mt per year. The company produces sheet metal for either onward supply to tertiary manufacturers of construction materials such as Metalex, Domod, Pioneer Aluminium Factory and Ghana Aluminium Company, or for the production of materials for the housing (e.g. roofing sheets, water tanks and louvre blades), household (e.g. hollowware and basins) and transport industries in Ghana.

Organization and management. As a public limited liability company listed on the Ghana Stock Exchange, Aluworks has a board of directors principally appointed by the various institutional shareholders. This process is undertaken once every year by rotation. The six-member board provides guidance and oversight to the company. The board's responsibility is to set the company's strategic direction, to monitor the activities of the executive management and to present a balanced and understandable assessment of the company's progress and prospects for the future. This information directly affects the share price of the company.

The board oversees a management team headed by the managing director. The management team is at liberty to take decisions that will benefit the company. There are sectional managers who report to the management team and who oversee the supervisors and other junior staff.

The company currently has about 270 employees and enjoys autonomy in all aspects of its operations with no external pressures.

Firm capabilities. As an ISO certified company, Aluworks produces to international standards and is well known on the market for its quality. Despite competition from low-price imported materials from China, the company has not compromised on quality, instead striving to maintain quality at prices that are affordable for the tertiary manufacturers and customers.

Competition. Despite its manufacturing monopoly, Aluworks faces strong competition from Chinese products. As a response to this competition, Aluworks continues to innovate. An example of this is the recent introduction of roofing sheets in various new shapes and colours to its product range. The company is very flexible, producing customized products to the specifications of customers if orders meet a minimum threshold.

Supply and marketing chain. VALCO was the main source of ingots until it closed down in the late 1990s. Aluworks then began to import supplies from Jamaica but the prices were about 40% higher than VALCO's. With VALCO's reactivation, Aluworks's input costs have been cut by almost 36%. This has helped it to boost its sales.

The company produces to order. The supply process begins with the procurement department sourcing aluminium ingots, spare parts, additives and paint. The sales and marketing department is instrumental in bringing in customer orders and new business.

Once orders are received, production begins. The imported ingots are smelted and held in furnaces at high temperatures and under high pressures; strict quality control is observed. The molten ingots are then poured into casts of different widths. After casting it goes into cold rolling, a process that reduces the width from the original 0.6 mm to 0.5 mm, 0.4 mm and so on, according to customer specifications. The rolls are then subjected to tension levelling and then painted and dried. The finished products are stored in coils for onward transportation to their destinations or to the ports for export.

Exports. Aluworks exports about 45% of its finished products to other countries within the West African subregion, especially Nigeria, which is currently its biggest market. The company also exports to secondary markets in the US, the Caribbean and Europe.

Development agenda. Aluworks's development agenda is to strengthen its market base in West Africa. The company intends to install new machinery and to add a paint line to expand its range of colours.

12.2.3   Tema Steel Company Limited

Basic details. Built in 1974, Tema Steel is one of four Ghanaian companies that produce rebar for the construction industry from locally sourced scrap steel. The company also operates a foundry on its site, which produces some castings for the mining industry. This accounts for about a quarter of the company's turnover.

Tema Steel has an annual melting capacity of 45,000 mt and an output of 33,000 mt. Its rolling capacity is 50,000 mt per annum with current annual output running at 36,000 mt.

The company employs between 650 and 700 people (including permanent and contract staff) and has a current turnover of US$30 million per annum.

History. The company's production plant was initially built for the government-owned Kwame Nkrumah Steel Works in 1974–75. The government-owned concern stopped operating towards the end of the 1980s and was divested by the government in 1991. It was purchased following a bidding process by its present owners, a multinational group headed by M. J. Patel and Prasad Motaparti. M. J. Patel currently acts as the director of the company, which was renamed as Tema Steel Company Limited.

Prior to his involvement at Tema Steel M. J. Patel had been based in Kenya, where he ran a sawmill and a timber products company as well as a unit assembling electrical switches.

M. J. Patel and Prasad Motaparti's business group currently operates across several countries. Besides their Kenyan interest they own two companies in India: Toshali Cements and Martu Pearl. They also operate in the Ukraine and have cement plants in Burkina Faso, Togo and Ethiopia (where they have just built an integrated cement plant with an annual capacity of 1 million mt, which comes online early in 2012). The group turnover is in excess of US$1 billion per year.

Current activities and products. The principal product of Tema Steel is rebar for the construction industry. The group's other Ghanaian companies are involved in the production of forgings for the mining industry (West Africa Forgings) and in the production of cement (Diamond Cement (Gh) Limited and Savannah Diamond Cement Limited (see Chapter 11)).

Tema Steel also operates a foundry on its site that produces some castings for the mining industry. This activity accounts for about a quarter of the company's turnover.

Firm capabilities. Prior to its takeover by Tema Steel in 1991, Kwame Nkrumah Steel Works had an annual capacity of 12,000 mt for melting and 20,000 mt for rolling but it never achieved an output of more than 6,500 mt in melting or 9,000 mt in rolling. Tema Steel currently has an annual melting capacity of 45,000 mt and an output of 33,000 mt. Its rolling capacity is 50,000 mt per annum and its current annual output is 36,000 mt.

Competition. Tema Steel has three competitors in the production of rebar from scrap steel: Special Steel, Ferro Fabrik and Western Steel and Forging. (One further company, Wahome, closed down recently and has just been acquired by a Chinese group that has renamed it Sentuo Steel Limited.)

Supply and marketing chain. The four firms in this industry all depend entirely on purchases of scrap steel from local scrap dealers, who deliver it directly to their plants. It would be uneconomic for them to import scrap steel. Current law prohibits the export of scrap steel from Ghana, but the law is not enforced and substantial shipments flow out of the country on a regular basis. This represents the main difficulty facing this group of companies.

Exports. Tema Steel exports small quantities of rebar to Burkina Faso and Mali.

Development agenda.   The company's, and the group's, recent expansion within Ghana has focused on its cement interest. This in part reflects the continuing concerns about the viability of the steel business in the face of illegal scrap export and high electricity prices.

12.2.4   *Ghana Metal Fabrication & Construction Limited*

Basic details.   This company and its older and smaller sister company, AEL Engineering Limited, are both owned by B. K. Amandi and are engaged in large-scale steel fabrications and in the processing and exporting of scrap aluminium, respectively. Ghana Metal Fabrications & Construction accounts for 70% of the group's turnover of US$2 million per annum. The two companies together employ 127 people.

History.   Amandi was born in Nigeria and came to Kumasi in the Ashanti region of Ghana in his teens. There, he came into contact with some Hausa people who were gathering scrap aluminium in villages near his home and then melting and casting it into aluminium ingots that could be sold on the market. Amandi became involved in this activity, smelting the scrap on his landlord's premises. He heard, after a time, that the Kaiser Aluminum company was disposing of waste (aluminium dust or 'dross') on their Accra site, and it was while scavenging on the site that he was discovered by an American employee of the Kaiser company[4] who was curious to discover what he was doing with the waste material.

The Kaiser employee came with five colleagues to inspect Amandi's operations and advised him that it was inappropriate to operate under such conditions. The accumulation of dross on the Kaiser site was a problem for the company as it attracted scavengers, and the six Kaiser executives gave Amandi a letter of support that allowed him to purchase an industrial plot and to put his operation on a sounder footing. In 1978 Amandi transformed his operation (which he had run since 1973 under the name Amandi Scraps and Pots Manufacturing Enterprise) into a limited liability company called Amandi Enterprises Limited, which he renamed Aluminium Enterprises Limited in 1980. In that same year he spent some time in the UK, first in Birmingham learning about smelting processes, and subsequently in other parts of England, Scotland and Wales where he was able to observe best-practice smelting operations.

---

[4] The US-based Kaiser company had been operating in Ghana under the name Volta Aluminum Company (VALCO) since 1965. See the company profile of Aluworks above.

On his return to Ghana he raised his yield on dross input from its former level of 25% to between 40% and 50%. He benefitted from the advice and assistance of technicians in the Kaiser company who helped him to improve his operations. His output levels reached almost 500 mt per month, and he was selling to buyers from Mali, Burkina Faso and the Ivory Coast as well as to local makers of kitchen utensils. By 1980 he was employing 500 people and had an annual turnover of US$5–6 million. During this period he was buying 90% of all the scrap aluminium in Ghana and was the biggest smelter of scrap aluminium in West Africa.

By 1990 Amandi was regarded as one of Ghana's leading businessmen and had several approaches from international financial institutions that wanted to invest in his company. He eventually entered an arrangement with a European investment bank that involved a major investment to modernize his plant. The affair ended badly, however, and was followed by many years of litigation. He was deposed from his role in running the company and replaced by foreign consultants. He still retains his ownership of the business but it no longer smelts aluminium. Rather, it engages in the collection of scrap aluminium, which is compressed and exported.

In 1997 Amandi acquired an engineering operation, Ghana National Trading Corporation, that was being divested by the government of Ghana. This became a subsidiary of his AEL company and was named AEL Engineering Limited. In 2005 it was renamed Ghana Metal Fabrication & Construction Limited.

Current activities and products. Ghana Metal Fabrication & Construction designs and builds very large volume tanks and tank farms (i.e. large sets of tanks), principally for use in the oil and gas industry. The firm also fabricates underground and surface storage tanks, vertical and horizontal storage tanks, bulk tankers, telecommunication towers, light and sign poles, metal kiosks and containers, multi-module fuel station canopies, feeder canopies, steel trusses, silos, metal platforms, flatbed articulator bodies, sided articulator bodies, and bullion van bodies. It is also engaged in pipe fitting and welding as well as supplying other technical and civil construction services.

The company also provides consulting services, helping firms develop their business plans in order to raise finance to support an extension of their activities in oil and gas storage.

Ghana Metal Fabrications & Construction supplies a number of blue-chip companies, mostly in the oil and gas sector. Its main clients are Shell Oil Ghana Limited, Mobil (now Total Fina Elf), Ghana Oil Company, Engen, Havilla Oil Ghana Limited, Glory Oil Ghana Limited and Fraga Oil

Ghana Limited. The company also supplies the Coca Cola Company, Accra Brewery Limited and Ghana Oil Development Company Limited with a wide range of metal fabrication products, such as overhead tanks, storage tanks, masts, billboards, and so on.

Organization and management. Ghana Metal Fabrications & Construction has a management board to which Amandi, as CEO, reports. Four function heads (general managers) are responsible for operations, administration, marketing and internal audit control. Under the function head for operations, four managers take responsibility for project management, fabrication yard/equipment, project planning and quality assurance.

Firm capabilities. The most valuable capabilities of the company fall into three specialized areas.

Pipe laying. This covers large-scale transport pipe projects and the establishment of connections to oil and gas facilities. The company guarantees top-quality execution of pipe laying contracts, whether the systems are above ground or underground. Ghana Metal Fabrications & Construction meets highly specialized technical specifications in oil rigging, manifolds and heated fuel oil circuits for the chemical, petrochemical and other sectors.

Facility revamp and upgrade. The company executes projects for the rehabilitation and upgrade of flow station facilities in gas/liquid/solid separation. Working with international firms, the company delivers weirs, antifoam baffles, plate packs for liquid/liquid coalescing, desand jets, gas outlet vanes, demister mist extractors and wave baffles.

Foundation bundwall design and construction. Ghana Metal Fabrications & Construction utilizes piled foundations in which the superstructure loads are transferred to more competent bearing stratum at depth. It also undertakes the construction of bundwalls for spillage containment, all its bundwalls being well compacted and reinforced with wire mesh to withstand the effect of shocks, blows and contractions.

Competition. Ghana Metal Fabrications & Construction is the market leader in undertaking fabrications for the oil and gas sector. There are three medium-sized companies in this segment of the steel industry that also manufacture some of the products made by Ghana Metal Fabrications & Construction. One such company is Pacifictord Metal Works & Trading Enterprise, established in the 1970s, which fabricates a wide range of products including roller shutters, custom fabrication, collapsible doors and windows, aluminium windows, trusses for buildings and advertising billboards.

Ghana Metal Fabrications & Construction faces competition in some areas from the many small enterprises engaged in metal fabrications. Most of these companies manufacture basic products such as metal gates, signposts, window reinforcements, security doors, cabinets, garden chairs, children's playground facilities, vehicle body parts and metal tubes.

Supply and marketing chain.   The company imports the steel used in its tanks from Belgium and the Ukraine. Its customers for tanks and tank farms include most of the oil and gas majors operating in Ghana, as well as major companies outside the oil and gas sector (such as palm oil producers and leading beverage companies). It is estimated that 80% of the tanks sourced in Ghana by the domestic oil industry are sourced from the company Ghana Metal Fabrications & Construction.

Development agenda.   As the oil industry expands in Ghana over the next few years, the level of demand for heavy steel fabrication will grow very rapidly. Ghana Metal Fabrications & Construction has already entered into a profit-sharing joint venture agreement with a leading Nigerian metal fabricator that has had extensive experience in both tank and pipeline construction. The company is also considering a possible joint venture agreement with an Indian firm that has extensive experience in large-scale pipelines and in the building of terminals for the industry.

12.2.5   Wire Weaving Industries (Ghana) Limited

Basic details.   Wire Weaving Industries is a producer of drawn wire products. It was established in 1965 and delivered its first products in September 1969.

The company employs 100 people and its turnover was US$6 million in 2010.

History.   Wire Weaving Industries was one of three companies founded by four partners, two of whom came from Lebanon. Two of the four partners were traders and two had a technical and engineering background. The other two companies founded by the partners, Azar Chemical Industries Limited and City Paints, are both involved in paint manufacturing and are also still in operation.

The drawn wire business was acquired in 1992 by its two present owners. One of these owners, Yasser Aschkar, who is the current managing director of the company, previously had a franchise to manufacture paint from a UK multinational.

Current activities and products. Wire Weaving Industries manufactures a wide range of wire products, including hexagonal wire netting, barbed wire, expanded metal, boundary master chain link, link fencing, razor wire and various types of wire mesh. The company serves a wide range of consumer needs in several sectors, including building contractors, infrastructure developers, farmers, fishermen and the agro-industrial sector, especially the poultry industry.

Organization and management. The company has a three-member board of directors. The management team is headed by the managing director, Aschkar, who is supported by functional heads with responsibilities for production, marketing, finance and administration and quality assurance.

Firm capabilities. Wire Weaving Industries is not currently involved in wire drawing or in galvanizing. All companies in the drawn wire business import ready-coated wire as their raw material.

In September 2011 Wire Weaving Industries obtained ISO 9001:2008 certification.

Competition. The company's direct competitors are B5 Plus Limited and United Steel, each of which makes some products that overlap with the product range of Wire Weaving Industries. United Steel makes hollow squares and round pipes from imported steel sheet sourced from the Ukraine, Russia and China.

Supply and marketing chain. Wire Weaving Industries imports ready-coated wire from South Africa, Brazil and China.

Exports. The company exports small volumes to Togo, Benin and occasionally to Nigeria.

Developmental agenda. The company is currently planning to expand its operations into wire drawing. This would involve a dry drawing process on non-galvanized bar.[5]

---

[5] To make a galvanizing operation economically viable, a minimum annual output of around 5,000 mt would be required, which far exceeds the current output level of Wire Weaving Industries.

12.2.6 Nexans Kabelmetal (Ghana) Limited

Basic details. Manufacturing in more than 20 countries, Nexans is a global expert in cables and cabling systems and an international leader in the industry. In Ghana the group is represented by the subsidiary company Nexans Kabelmetal (Ghana) Limited, which is the leading cable manufacturer in Ghana and was the first in West Africa.

The company is located in the Tema heavy industrial area, a suburb of Accra, and has a staff strength of 107, all of whom are permanent. The turnover of Nexans in 2010 was approximately US$19 million.

History. A feasibility study was conducted in 1970 by a German company, Planungsgruppe Juergen Richter, with the backing of the National Investment Bank of Ghana, which also involved Kabel und Metalwerke (Kabelmetal) of Hanover, Germany. It was recommended that wire drawing and cable manufacture would be a viable enterprise in Ghana. The establishment of Nexans Kabelmetal (Ghana) Limited was the result, and on 31 July 1971 the company opened its first plant. The idea was a welcome one and it helped to drive the government's development agenda. At the time of opening the first plant, the Electricity Company of Ghana owned 24% of the company's shares, the National Investment Bank owned 25% and Kabelmetal owned 51%.

The company operated as Kabelmetal from 1968 to 2002, when the name was changed to Alcatel on the company's acquisition by a French company. However, as Kabelmetal's brand was a well-known one, Alcatel maintained it in their registered name: Alcatel Kabelmetal Ghana Limited.

Nexans took over from Alcatel in 2004, choosing to stick with the name Kabelmetal in its registered name: Nexans Kabelmetal (Ghana) Limited.

Current activities and products. Nexans is an ISO certified company and its core business is the manufacture of cables and cabling systems for the following four sectors: energy, industrial, construction and telephony. The cables for these sectors are all produced in Ghana. The products are as follows:

- surface wiring cables, multi-core (PVC insulated and PVC sheathed multi-core cables with solid and stranded copper conductors),
- surface wiring cables, single-core (PVC insulated and PVC sheathed single-core cables with solid and stranded copper conductors),
- flexible flat cords (for use in dry rooms for small hand-held appliances and loudspeakers),

- PVC insulated consumer connection copper cables (PVC insulated single-core cables with stranded hard drawn copper conductors 1,100 V),
- stranded copper conductors,
- mains cables, single-core and multi-core,
- jumper wires,
- internal wiring flexible cables,
- garden hoses,
- internal telephone cables,
- flexible round cords,
- conduit house wiring cables,
- binding and earth wires,
- bare copper conductors,
- armoured underground cables,
- bare aluminium conductors,
- aerial bundled conductors,
- aluminium overhead conductors.

Organization and management. Nexans is headed by a country manager and a managing director, who are supported by various line managers. The company has a five-member board of directors.

Firm capabilities. As a member of a group with a worldwide presence, the sheer size of Nexans places it at an advantage over its competitors. It has a well-structured research and development centre that is supported by its worldwide presence; this ensures that the quality of its products remains at the top of the range. With over 40 years' experience, Nexans is capable of producing any type of cable or conductor within its production programme at short notice.

Competition. The company's current competitors are Tropical Cable and Conductor Limited, Reroy Cables and imports from China and elsewhere. Regulation of the industry is not tight and access to the market is easy. Nexans is embarking on new marketing efforts to address the situation.

Supply and marketing chain. Aluminium and copper are imported from France, Vietnam and Oman. The copper arrives at the port in rolls and is then transported to the warehouses for quality control tests.

Nexans has distribution centres in almost all the regional capitals.

Exports. The company exports about 5% of its products to Burkina Faso.

Recent developments. Nexans aims to expand production through the installation of new machinery and the launch of new products onto the market. This has already begun with the installation of a new machine, the drum twister armouring machine, which has allowed the company to add armoured cables to its product range.

Chapter 13

PHARMACEUTICALS

13.1 Sector Profile

Background and overview. There are about 50 pharmaceutical companies registered with the Ghana Pharmacy Council. These companies import active ingredients and formulate and package tablets, syrups, capsules and intravenous fluids. Most manufacturers are also involved in the direct importation of final pharmaceutical products.

Structure of the industry.

Manufacturing. Among the leading pharmaceutical manufacturers in Ghana are Phyto-Riker (formerly GIHOC Pharmaceuticals), Dannex Company Ltd, Ernest Chemist Limited, Ayrton Drug Manufacturing Ltd, Letap Company Ltd, Starwin Limited, Intravenous Infusions Ltd, Bikkai, Major & Co., Pfizer and Starwin.

Wholesaling and distribution. Most of the manufacturing companies listed above are also wholesalers. For example, Ernest Chemist Limited has two wholesale outlets and is in the process of setting up a third. Most of the operators stock both local and imported products. Most wholesalers also sell at retail.

Retailing. Most retail outlets involve a single pharmacist or licensed chemical seller.

In the regional capitals, a pharmaceutical retail unit will be found within 1–2 km of every location. Units are open for not less than 10 hours per day and some operate a 24-hour service.

Supply and marketing chain. The pharmaceutical sector comprises manufacturers, wholesalers, distributors, retailers and consumers. Within this market, the government of Ghana is a major player, both as a regulator of the market and as a buyer involved directly in the wholesale supply of drugs and healthcare services to public healthcare institutions.

Distribution is undertaken by the distribution departments of the manufacturing companies. In addition to this, independent distributors buy in bulk and distribute products to retailers. The independent distributors are also importers and most have franchises from major international pharmaceutical manufacturers.

Policy context. Regulatory institutions include the Ministry of Health, the Pharmacy Council, the Ghana Standards Board and the Environmental Protection Agency. The Ministry of Health deals with policy formulation. The establishment of a pharmaceutical company requires licenses and permits from the Pharmacy Council, the Ministry of Health, the Ghana Standards Board and the Environmental Protection Agency.

Obtaining a license from the Pharmacy Council requires that steps are taken to satisfy World Health Organization guidelines for current good manufacturing practices. The Ghana Standards Board is responsible for quality evaluation: to ensure that all products in the country are safe. All manufacturers, importers and distributors are legally required to register with the Ghana Standards Board. The Environmental Protection Agency ensures that the manufacture, sale and use of pharmaceuticals meet strict environmental standards.

Challenges. A limited capacity to enforce regulations is a problem in the sector. Flaws in the public sector payment system and a weak public sector supply chain are also significant issues. A lack of working capital is a major cause of poor and unreliable supply arrangements by wholesalers. This is the result of the very low coverage of local production, which has resulted in a need to import from other countries to meet the country's needs. The high cost of inputs and the limited availability of qualified personnel are major challenges.

Competitiveness. About 70% of pharmaceutical products are imported, and competition among local manufacturers has intensified. Most are now upgrading their operations.

Demand status, trends and potential. Ghana imports about US$300 million worth of pharmaceutical products annually. Local manufacturers account for about a third of the total market. The market has been growing at about 10% annually.

Recent developments. Recent expansions in capacity have made Ghana one of the leading producers and distributors of medicine in West Africa. In November 2009, South Africa's largest drugs company, Adcock Ingram Holdings Ltd, bought a majority share in Ghana's leading pharmaceutical company, Ayrton Drug Manufacturing Ltd. In 2010, a US-based pharmaceutical company, Emerging World Pharma Inc., invested in setting up a facility in Sunyani to produce generic products. The company expects to start with 13 medicines and add another 18 products as production capacity expands.

The Food and Drugs Board and the Ghana Standards Board, through increased monitoring and surveillance, have been successful in detecting fake and unwholesome drugs, recently banning a number of companies whose products have failed to meet manufacturing standards. The two agencies have also banned the sale of several imported drugs that violate standards.

Profiles and lines of business of large firms.

Kama Health Services Limited was established in 1983 to manufacture drugs, operate animal and vegetable farms to source protein and vitamins, and to operate a clinic and offer management consultancy on health services. It is profiled in the next section.

Phyto-Riker (GIHOC) Pharmaceuticals Limited produces a wide range of essential drugs used in West Africa. These include anti-inflammatory and anti-pyretic drugs, analgesics and anti-infective agents, especially antibiotics and anti-malarials, as well as drugs used for the treatment of common tropical diseases. The company is profiled in the next section.

Dannex Ghana Limited is the fourth-largest producer in the industry and has revived its fortunes following a restructuring of the company in 2004. It is profiled in the next section.

Capital 02, a leading producer of herbal medicines, is profiled in the next section.

A medium-sized firm: Tobinco Pharmaceuticals Limited. Tobinco Pharmaceuticals is a private Ghanaian company that was founded in 1984 as Tobinco Company Limited by Samuel Amo Tobbin. Tobbin started in business selling pharmaceutical drugs (which he purchased from drug stores) to companies and individuals at a markup. He sold the products around Takoradi, Bogosu, Tarkwa and Prestea in the Western region of Ghana and in Akropong in the Eastern region. After two years of trading, Tobbin formalized his business by printing invoices and receipts to cover sales made to companies, despite the fact that he was operating without being a registered business. He wound up the business and travelled to Japan in 1989, returning to Ghana several years later to continue his business.

Six months after his return, Tobbin received a call from a prospective supplier in India, S. N. Kamath of Bliss GVS, who had decided to try him as a possible business partner. Kamath started by shipping four cartons of anti-malarial drugs to Tobbin in Ghana. Further business followed and Kamath came to Ghana in 2002 to meet his new business partner.

Tobinco Pharmaceuticals now imports pharmaceutical products mainly from India, the principal suppliers being Bliss GVS, Ally Pharma and Blue Map. The company has a nationwide distribution network that allows it to cover all parts of the country. This has played an important role in the success of the company.

The company now aims to set up a factory to commence manufacturing pharmaceutical products itself. Tobinco Pharmaceuticals also aims to expand its reach into the West African subregion.

Rationale for selecting profiled firms. Kama Industries Limited is among the three largest pharmaceutical manufacturing companies in the country. Phyto-Riker is the only ISO certified pharmaceutical manufacturer in Ghana. Dannex, one of the top ten pharmaceutical manufacturers in Ghana, offers an example of how restructuring and strategic partnership can turn around an ailing pharmaceutical establishment. Capital 02 provides an example of local success in the sale of herbal medicines.

13.2   Profiles of Major Firms

13.2.1   *Kama Health Services Limited*

Basic details.   The Kama Health Services group of companies employs 250 people and had an annual turnover US$12.5 million in 2010.

History.   The origin of the company can be traced back to the establishment of Kama Health Services in 1983 by Dr Michael Agyekum Addo. The business started with the opening of a pharmacy by the founder in Kumasi in the Ashanti region. Because of difficulties in raising the requisite capital to start his business, all the inputs needed to commence operations were bought using credit (rent, furnishings and stock). In 1986, he began manufacturing products in his garage.

Kama Health Services now has 11 outlet pharmacies in six regions in Ghana and currently represents eight multinational manufacturing companies. The staff strength of the company increased from one in 1983 to 150 in 2000 and to 250 in 2010.

Current activities and products. Kama Industries manufactures medicines for both the local and international markets. The company produces 42 different types of syrups, suspensions and mixtures, 10 kinds of tablet, 7 kinds of capsule and 1 powder product.

Organization and management. The Kama group is headed by an eight-member board of directors, comprising six Ghanaians and two Dutch nationals, to which the CEO reports. The deputy CEO supervises administration, production, marketing and accounts.

Firm capabilities. Kama employs a number of both local and expatriate professionals, who have extensive technical expertise in the pharmaceutical sector. Among these professionals are pharmacists who together have over 20 years' combined industry experience, which helps the company adhere to good manufacturing practice standards and to good distribution practice standards.

Kama uses state-of-the-art technology, enabling it to meet its target requirements in both the local and subregional markets. The plant comprises four 3,000 litre tanks, a bottle washing section, a production section, and filing and packaging sections.

Kama invests in market research, through which it gathers strategic market information to help it with is product development and innovation. This contributes to relative growth in the market of the company.

The success of Kama has been attributed to a number of factors, one of which is the pragmatic leadership that has transformed the company from a small entity into a big player in the pharmaceutical industry in Ghana in 20 years. From a humble beginning – buying stock on credit – and a turnover of under US$1,200 in 1983, the annual sales revenue of the company reached US$4.9 million in 2000 and over US$12.5 million in 2010.

Competition. Kama's key competitors are Ernest Chemist Limited, Dannex Limited, Kina Pharma, Phyto-Riker, Ayrton Limited and Starwin. Most of these companies compete with Kama in all three segments of the market: manufacturing, wholesale and retail.

Kama also faces competition from a large range of imported generic products. Ghana currently imports about 60% of its total pharmaceutical needs.

Supply and marketing chain. Kama imports its main inputs, including ingredients, intermediate products and packaging materials, from India and the Netherlands. Materials are sent to the quality control department on arrival for screening, to ensure that there are no defects in the inputs to the production process and to guarantee final product quality.

As well as having its own distribution and retail business, Kama relies on selected pharmaceutical distributors.

Exports. Kama currently exports 10% of its total production volume to Liberia, Sierra Leone and Nigeria.

13.2.2   Phyto-Riker (GIHOC) Pharmaceuticals Limited

Basic details. Phyto-Riker (GIHOC) Pharmaceuticals was established in 1998 when the state-owned Ghana Industrial Holding Corporation (GIHOC) Pharmaceuticals was acquired by Phyto-Riker Pharmaceuticals Incorporated through a competitive privatization process. The factory is located close to Accra. The company employs 200 people, including 30 casuals who work mainly in packaging.

History. GIHOC Pharmaceuticals was set up in 1962 as part of the country's industrialization drive by the first president of the Republic of Ghana, Dr Kwame Nkrumah.

Run by Ghanaian management and technical staff, the company was supported by the United Nations Industrial Development Organization (UNIDO), which offered technical expertise in production, quality control and plant maintenance between 1971 and 1974. UNIDO also arranged refresher courses for technical staff. Although capacity utilization and total output were low under state ownership, GIHOC products maintained a strong reputation for quality.

In 1991, GIHOC Pharmaceuticals was divested and sold to the American pharmaceutical company, Phyto-Riker Incorporated, which chose to retain the GIHOC name. The company registered with the Ghana Free Zones Board, under which they enjoyed tax rebates and concessions as an exporting company, selling 70% or more of their output outside Ghana.

During this period, Phyto-Riker's major market was in Francophone West Africa, where it sold through a French agent. However, following a change in management, a new managing director decided to change the export orientation of the company in the direction of Anglophone countries. This resulted in a dispute between the French agent and the company, eventually leading to the termination of their contract.

Following these developments the company experienced poor financial results, and in 2004 Phyto-Riker Incorporated decided to sell its interests to Ghanaian private investors. Databank currently holds 90% of the company's shares, with the government of Ghana holding the remaining 10%. The name Phyto-Riker has been maintained by the new owners.

Current activities and products. Phyto-Riker is the only ISO certified pharmaceutical manufacturing company in Ghana. The company produces a wide range of branded and generic products: syrups (paracetamol, amodiaquine, cotrimoxazole), antacids (aluminium hydroxide, magisil), analgesics (aspirin, ibuprofen), antibacterials/antinfectives (amoxicillin, ciproflaxacin), antimalarials, anti-allergy medications and psychotherapeutics.

Organization and management. Phyto-Riker has a board of directors to whom the heads of various divisions (finance and administration, manufacturing, quality assurance, sales and marketing, and product development and regulatory) report.

Firm capabilities. The company's well-equipped laboratory undergoes strict annual quality audits from ISO personnel.

A solid environmental protection standard ensures that all waste is properly disposed of.

Competition. Despite facing increased competition from imported pharmaceutical products from China and India, the company has been able to maintain its domestic position as a result of the recognized quality of its products. Some pharmacies and hospitals have a strong preferences for Phyto-Riker products over other locally manufactured or imported products.

Supply and marketing chain. Active ingredients (salicylic acid, malarone, etc.) are imported in bulk in powdered or granulated form from India and are then manufactured into tablet form and packed in bubble packs for distribution.

The company does not have any branches for direct sales. All sales are through wholesales and retailers.

Exports. Phyto-Riker exports to Nigeria and other West African countries.

Development agenda. In 2010, Phyto-Riker secured new contracts that have helped boost the company's capacity utilization.

The firm's goal is to list on the Ghana Stock Exchange within the next five years.

13.2.3 Dannex Ghana Limited

Basic details. Dannex is a limited liability company incorporated in 1964 under the Ghana Companies Code of 1963 (Act 179). The company was originally incorporated as Danafco Manufacturing Limited. The name was changed to Dumex Limited in 1965 and subsequently to Dannex Ghana Limited in 1992 when the foreign partner, Dumex Limited of Denmark, sold its shares to the government and ceased to be a shareholder in the company.

With an annual revenue of US$4 million (2011), Dannex employs 170 people.

History. In the early 1960s a Danish business entrepreneur, B. A. Hydeman, formed a partnership with a group of other entrepreneurs to manufacture plastics. In 1965, Dumex AS of Denmark, a global pharmaceutical manufacturing firm, merged with the company to manufacture pharmaceutical products in Ghana.

The operations of the company were divided into two distinct but interrelated functions: manufacturing and distribution. The manufacturing aspect of the business operated under the name Dumex Limited and the distribution aspect operated under the name Danafco Limited. The company was incorporated at a time when the government of Ghana was promoting the rapid industrialization of the Ghanaian economy in the 1960s. In response to this, the company focused mainly on manufacturing and all its products were sold exclusively through its sister company, Danafco. The exclusive sole distributorship of Danafco ended in 1995.

As the pharmaceutical industry grew and became more competitive, new manufacturers and major distributors and importers entered the industry. Most distributors imported pharmaceutical products from Europe and Asia. Dannex's market share started to decrease and simultaneously the company faced a number of management problems that contributed to a decline in its fortunes. The company was eventually divested by the government of Ghana.

In 2000 a group of Ghanaian investors, ECA Investment Holdings, took over the ailing company by buying 80% of the shareholding, with the remaining 20% held by the government of Ghana. The strategic takeover was followed by a restructuring of the company's operations in 2005, which was led by an expert contracted by the strategic investor, ECA.

Current activities and products. Dannex currently manufactures 24 different kinds of off-patent, generic products in two broad product groups: health and beauty. Under the health product group, Dannex produces painkillers, stimulants (i.e. blood tonics), analgesics and veterinary products. The range of beauty products comprises hair products (pomades) and skin lotions for both adults and infants.

Organization and management. The organization of Dannex is structured around five core functional areas: production, human resources, quality control, finance and administration, and marketing. The managing director reports to the board of directors.

Firm capabilities. The core activity of Dannex lies in the production of health and beauty products. High product quality has been achieved through significant investment in staff training.

Competition. Many distributors have integrated upwards into manufacturing, increasing competition for all companies in the industry.

The Food and Drugs Board of Ghana has, over the past two years, clamped down on importers of performance-enhancing drugs and expired products, which has helped to improve the sales of local pharmaceutical firms such as Dannex.

Supply and marketing chain. The active ingredients in Dannex's products are currently imported from Asia (especially from China and India). Upon arrival these products are sent to the company's laboratories for inspection and quality-assurance tests. After passing all quality-assurance tests, production begins – packaging and labelling follow later. The finished products are sent back to the laboratory and random samples are inspected for quality. After this last quality check, the products are transported to warehouses for marketing and distribution.

In addition to its Accra operation, Dannex has several distribution centres in Kumasi and Takoradi from which supplies are sent to the middle, northern and western parts of the country.

The company sells to government hospitals, clinics and health posts throughout the country as well as to regional medical pharmacies. Its turnover has increased from US\$3.5 million in 2010 to US\$4 million in 2011.

Exports. Dannex does not currently export.

Development agenda. Dannex plans to introduce various new products in the next five years.

13.2.4 Capital O2 Limited

Basic details. Capital O2 is one of the largest manufacturers of natural health products in Ghana. Located at Dansoman, one of Accra's suburbs, the company has a staff strength of 200 of which 160 are permanent. The annual turnover of the company was about US$1.5 million in 2010.

History.   Capital O2 was established by John Daniel Otoo in 1991. Prior to setting up the company, Otoo was a public servant and the shipping manager for the Ghana National Procurement Agency, where he worked for 19 years. In 1991 he began to import natural health products, and later began manufacturing products locally.

Otoo's decision to become involved in the industry was born out of his personal experience of using natural remedies for a chronic stomach ailment.

Current activities and products.   The company's brands include Living Bitters, which is a colon cleanser and is the flagship product of the company; Great Swedish Bitters, for blood circulation; Female Correction Formula, which is used for conditions affecting women, such as menstrual cycle disorders; Pawa O2, used for premature ejaculation and performance enhancement; and Malarials. Capital O2 manufactures over 20 different types of herbal remedy, treating typhoid fever, asthma and fibroids, as well as producing drugs to increase mental alertness and herbal products for the detoxification of the body.

In addition to the above products, Capital O2 produces bottled water (Aqua O2) and provides services including detoxification techniques, health education and counselling, and massage therapy. The company has an ultramodern, well-equipped natural health clinic with a team of professionals and trained specialists.

Organization and management.   The CEO, Otoo, reports to a seven-member board. The management team comprises the managing director, the general manager and five heads of departments.

Firm capabilities.   Capital O2 emphasizes quality assurance across the production cycle. The company won the International Star for Leadership in Quality award from Business Initiative Directions, France, in April 2011. The company also won the best practice award from the European Society for Quality Research in 2011.

Competition.   Capital O2's main competitors are medium- to large-scale herbal manufacturing companies: Champion Divine Clinic, Agbeve Herbal Clinic and Amen Scientific Herbal Hospital. A large number of small-scale manufacturers also offer herbal products.

Supply and marketing chain.   Herbs are almost all sourced locally. Packaging materials and labels are purchased locally. The company imports concentrates, corks and small quantities of herbs from South Africa, the UK, Switzerland and Germany. The company has nine offices in the Greater Accra region, three in the Ashanti region and one each in the Central, Brong Ahafo and Eastern regions. The company is also registered in the US, the UK, Equatorial Guinea, Angola and Nigeria.

The company has outlets in all the regional capitals. Its products are widely available in pharmacies throughout Ghana.

Exports.   The company has accredited agents through which it markets its products in the US, Europe and other African countries.

Challenges.   Capital O2's main concern is with the timescale (3–5 months) and complexity of processes for registering new products. The cost of registering products has increased in recent years. Natural health medicines do not appear on the accepted list of drugs prescribed under the National Health Insurance Scheme.

Development agenda.   Capital O2 aims to further expand its product range. The company also aims to expand its sales in Western and Southern Africa by adding fruit juices, natural drinks and chocolate drinks to its product range. In the long term, the company will consider setting up a School of Natural Health to train practitioners in natural healthcare.

Chapter 14

CHEMICALS

14.1 Sector Profile

Background and overview. The chemical industry produces basic chemicals, petrochemicals, fertilizers, paints, gases, pharmaceuticals and dyes. The sector covers over 70,000 commercial products and employs almost 25% of Ghana's industrial workforce.

Almost all inputs are imported. The main imports include petroleum products, fertilizers, pesticides and chemicals for the mining industry. Over 70% of the chemicals are used in agriculture (fertilizers and pesticides), the processing/manufacturing industries (mining, cement, metal, soap, textile, etc.) and the petroleum industry (oil refinery products and lubricants). About 20% of the imported chemicals are processed or repackaged for sale on the local market.[1]

Structure of the industry. The chemical industry comprises six segments.

- The polymers segment: polyethylene; polyvinyl chloride; polypropylene; polystyrene; man-made fibres including polyester, nylon and acrylic.
- The petrochemicals segment: bulk petrochemicals and intermediates made from liquefied petroleum gas, natural gas and crude oil. These include solvents (such as paint thinner), paints, drugs, fertilizers, pesticides, explosives, synthetic fibres and rubbers, flooring and insulating materials, compact discs, video tapes, electronic equipment and furniture.
- The inorganic chemicals segment: salt, chlorine, caustic soda, soda ash, nitric acid, phosphoric acid, sulphuric acid, titanium dioxide and hydrogen peroxide.

[1] Large quantities of mine tailings and inorganic pollutants such as arsenic, mercury, cyanide and oxides of sulphur are generated as waste. However, no waste is either imported into or exported out of the country. (Acquah, P. C. 1997. *National Profile to Assess the Chemicals Management Infrastructure in Ghana.* Environmental Protection Agency, Accra, Ghana.)

- The life sciences segment: chemical and biological substances, pharmaceuticals, diagnostics, animal health products and vitamins.
- The specialty chemicals segment: electrochemicals, industrial gases, adhesives and sealants, coatings, industrial and institutional cleaning chemicals and cyanide for mining activities.
- The consumer chemicals segment: soaps, detergents and cosmetics.
- Organic and inorganic fertilizers.

Plastics, salt production and pharmaceuticals are profiled in other chapters. This chapter focuses on paints, consumer goods and petrochemicals.

Supply and marketing chain.   The primary sources for imported chemicals are Germany, the UK, South Africa, the US, Japan, the Netherlands, Belgium, China, South East Asia and Nigeria. Over the past decade there has been a major shift away from suppliers in the US and Europe in favour of ones in Asia, and especially China, which is now the leading supplier.

A large variety of imported final products compete with locally produced chemicals.

While some companies have direct supply arrangements with parent companies, others buy through agents. Some, including Bamson Company Limited, have established a network of depots and distributors.

Policy context.   Given the diverse nature of the industry, different policies apply to each of the six key segments.[2] The Ghana Food and Drugs Board, the Environmental Protection Agency, the Ministry of Environment, Science & Technology, the Ghana Standards Board, the Ghana Atomic Energy Commission, the Hazardous Chemicals Committee, the Ministry of Health and the Plant Protection and Regulatory Services Directorate of the Ministry of Food and Agriculture all play roles in the formation and implementation of policies.

The Environmental Protection Agency is being strengthened through capacity development and through provision of equipment and financial resources. Liquid effluent emanating from industrial plants is often discharged without pre-treatment into water bodies resulting in heavy pollution: for example, Chemu Lagoon in the Tema area, and Korle Lagoon and the Odaw river in the Accra area. In the mining areas (the Western and Ashanti regions), various chemicals employed in the mining industry pollute water bodies, vegetation, soil and harm marine life. Gaseous emissions from both manufacturing and the mining industry are also of concern.

[2] See the chapters on textiles and garments (Chapter 8), pharmaceuticals (Chapter 13) and plastics and rubber (Chapter 15).

Challenges.   The current influx of low-price imported products onto the local market is making it very difficult for local companies to compete. Inadequate enforcement of regulations can allow unregistered products onto the local market, posing risks to consumers. Ghana currently lacks comprehensive legislation in this area, though the Environmental Protection Agency has, since 1989, been developing Chemical Import Procedures that cover consumer, industrial and agricultural chemicals.

Export status, strength and potential.   Most companies export to other countries in West Africa. Latex Foam Rubber Products Limited exports significant volumes to Nigeria, Togo, Burkina Faso and Ivory Coast. Others, such as the paint manufacturer Azar Chemical Industries Limited, export to Nigeria, Togo and Burkina Faso.

Recent developments.   With the recent developments in the commercial production of crude oil in Ghana, the oil and gas industry, together with the country's salt industry, is expected to provide a base for the establishment of a major petrochemical and integrated chloroalkali industry in the country.

Profiles and lines of business of large and medium-sized firms.   In the next section we profile five of the sector's leading firms: Azar Chemical Industries Limited, Bamson Company Limited, BBC Industrial Company (Ghana) Ltd (all in the paints sector), PZ Cussons (soaps, cosmetics and toiletries) and Bas van Buuren Ghana Limited (fertilizers). Here, we look at the history of a typical medium-sized firm: Appiah Menka Complex Limited.

Appiah Menka Complex was founded and is owned by Akenten Kweku Appiah Menka. The company produces soaps and vegetable oils for export to neighbouring West African countries. Appiah Menka Complex currently employs 70 people and has a production turnover of 40 mt of oil and 4 mt of soap per day.

Appiah Menka Complex dates back to the late 1960s when a lawyer, Akenten Kweku Appiah Menka, met a market woman who dealt in oil palm and who complained to him of difficulties in getting regular supplies. In 1969 he decided to venture into oil palm farming. He purchased 162 hectares of land and went to the National Investment Bank for a loan of GH¢4,500 to purchase oil palm seedlings from the Agricultural Extension Officers at the Ministry of Food and Agriculture. In 1969 he went into politics and joined the Progress Party, going on to serve as one of Ghana's ministers in the second republic. Following a spell in politics (and the confiscation, and subsequent return, of his business), in 1974 he obtained a loan of GH¢18,000 to purchase a palm oil mill to establish the Ashanti Oil Palm business.

Ashanti Oil Palm's production volumes were soon higher than the demand from the market women he supplied. After trying unsuccessfully to secure supply contracts with companies such as Lever Brothers (now Unilever Ghana Limited), he decided to go into making soap from the excess palm oil produced from his mill. Appiah Menka sought help from the German embassy to provide him with information and with assistance to purchase soap-making equipment from Weber and Seallander.

In 1977 Appiah Menka Complex was established to manufacture soap. The company's first product was a cake soap with the brand name Apino Soap. In 1992 the company introduced a second product, King Soap, onto the market.

Appiah Menka Complex currently produces vegetable oil and soap for export to Niger, Mali and Burkina Faso.

Rationale for selecting profiled firms. Azar Chemical Industries Limited is one of the oldest paint manufacturers in Ghana. Bamson Company Limited is the leading indigenous paint company and was a pioneer in the distribution and manufacture of car paints in Ghana. PZ Cussons Ghana Limited is the second largest producer of fast-moving consumer goods in Ghana. BBC Industrial Company (Ghana) Ltd is the largest local paint manufacturer. Bas van Buuren Ghana Limited pioneered the local production of natural fertilizer in Ghana.

14.2   Profiles of Major Firms

14.2.1   *Azar Chemical Industries Limited*

Basic details.   Azar Chemical Industries is a privately owned company that was established in 1968 to supply quality paints of all kinds to both the local and export markets. The company manufactures architectural and masonry paints, carpentry paints, and automotive and industrial paints. Situated in the North Kaneshie Industrial Area in Accra, the company has 300 employees and a group annual turnover of US$35 million.

History.   Azar Chemical Industries was founded by Elias Azar, a Lebanese entrepreneur, as a family business. The company initially operated under the name City Paints and traded in building materials and imported paints. The company began manufacturing paints in the 1980s, operating under the name Azar Chemical Industries. Azar Chemical Industries later became the Azar Group, comprising City Paints Supply Limited and Synrez Ghana

Limited. City Paints deals in paints and related products, while Synrez deals in the production of packaging products.

The company is currently run by two grandsons of the founder: Ghazi Azar, who is the managing director, and Rustom Azar, who is the executive director.

Current activities and products. The company manufacture paints of all kinds as well as related products. The first two products launched by the company, AzarTex Emulsion and Azar Gloss, have been very successful on the market and continue to be in high demand. The company produces three broad categories of paint for the architectural and masonry, carpentry and automotive sectors, under its Savana Paints, Azar Paints and Premium Paint brands. (The last category includes the Shield brand, which is specially formulated for use in harsh climatic conditions.) The group also produces Azar Tile Adhesive, Azar Lacquer and Azar Carpenter's Glue.

In addition to its core manufacturing work, the company also imports paint accessories, equipment and tools from Europe, the US and Turkey and sells them on the local market.

Organization and management. The management team comprises Rustom Azar (the executive director), Ghazi Azar (the managing director) Samuel Ato Christian (the director) and Rishi M. Lal (the financial controller). Line managers in charge of marketing, sales, transport, human resources, production and operations oversee the day-to-day activities of the company.

Firm capabilities. Azar Chemical Industries employs state-of-the-art Italian technology to produce a wide range of colour combinations as well as customized products. The company focuses on the production of high-quality products and provides excellent customer service. With 36 years' experience in the industry, Azar Chemical Industries has established a deep understanding of the domestic and regional markets. The company has a qualified and experienced workforce with the requisite technical training.

Competition. The company faces competition from imported paints from various countries including China and Israel. It also faces competition from local paint manufacturing companies such as Bamson Company and BBC Industrial Company (Ghana).

Supply and marketing chain. The company imports its main inputs, pigments, from Italy. The finished products are sold through retail shops/outlets, through the company's own showroom (City Paints), and through its own network of distributors across the country.

Exports.   The company currently exports its products to several countries within the West African subregion, including Togo, Burkina Faso and Nigeria.

Challenges.   The main issue facing the company is increased competition from imported paints, especially from China, which sell at relatively low prices.

Development agenda.   Azar Chemical Industries has plans to build up its export sales over the next five years. The company is scheduled to relocate to new offices on the Spintex Road in 2012.

14.2.2   Bamson Company Limited

Basic details.   Bamson Company is a privately owned Ghanaian company established in March 1980. The company is wholly Ghanaian owned and is the market leader in the manufacturing and distribution of car paint in Ghana. Bamson Company has a staff strength of 150 and an average annual turnover of US$3 million in car paints and US$1.5 million in house paints. The company's head office is located in the central business district of Accra.

History.   Bamson Company was founded in 1980 by Kwame Ofosu Bamfo, a Ghanaian entrepreneur. Originally a trader, he operated as Bamfo and Sons, a family business he ran with his brother and his son. The company sold local paints at retail and was one of the agents/retailers for GIHOC Paints (a division of the government-owned Ghana Industrial Holding Corporation, one of the largest local paint manufacturers at the time). Later that same year (1980), Bamson Company began importing car refinishing paints from Akzo Nobel, a Dutch multinational that manufactures a brand of paints called Sikkens. During this period, the sole local agent for Sikkens in Ghana was Reiss & Co., a Ghana-based distributor of chemical products and fertilizers. Bamson Company began importing Akzo Nobel paint products with permission from Reiss & Co., but three years later it became the new local agent for the Sikkens brand in Ghana – and it remains the sole agent for the Sikkens brand today. The company has won several awards for excellence in innovation and in customer service.

Current activities and products.   The company's products cover three categories of automobile paints (through two major brands, Sikkens and Dynacoat):

- high segment, mainly used for top-of-the-range cars such as Mercedes Benz;
- medium segment, mainly used for commercial vehicles and trucks; and
- low segment, mainly used for lower-end cars.

Bamson Company also produces household paints. The three types of paints produced for the household sector are Crown paint (decorative paint imported from the UK), Sandtex and Bamtex (which is locally formulated and manufactured by the company).

Bamson Company provides technical training to develop the capacities of garages, sprayers, artisans, painters and a broad spectrum of paint users in the appropriate handling and use of its products. This programme, which is provided free of charge to customers, has contributed to the company's strong brand positioning in the market.

Organization and management.   Bamson Company has a five-member board of directors chaired by the founder and owner, who is also the managing director. The company has a team of managers responsible for sales and marketing, production, finance and administration, operations and commercial.

Firm capabilities.   With over 25 years in the paint sector, Bamson Company has become synonymous with automobile paint in Ghana. The company produces to international quality standards. With its capacity to produce large volumes, it has been able to handle major projects such as the refurbishment of the country's international airport. Bamson Company supplies most of the automobile companies in Ghana with toners for car paints and has installed colour mixing equipment for automobile companies and garages. Its provision of technical training to paint users has contributed to its success; it has established two training schools in Accra and Kumasi and has trained over 10,000 sprayers.

Competition.   In the area of car paints, Bamson Company faces no serious competition at the high end of the market but it does face challenges at the low end from imported products, and especially from Chinese imports. The company faces competition in the house paints sector from two domestic competitors: Azar Chemical Industries and BBC Industrial Company (Ghana) (the makers of Leyland and Leylac paints).

Supply and marketing chain.   In the automobile paints sector, Bamson Company imports toners from Akzo Nobel for the production of up to

30,000 different shades of paint, as well as for producing customized products. The company then mixes the primary colours using automated equipment supplied by Akzo Nobel. The main inputs for paints for the housing sector (powders, binders and solvents) are imported from European countries including Belgium and Spain.

The company has six branches and 40 dealers and distributors throughout the country. The six branches are located in Agbogbloshie, Mataheko, Adabraka, Tudu, Tema in the south and Kumasi in the Ashanti region, which covers the northern half of the country. This ensures product availability throughout the country. The company works closely with major dealers and has a sponsorship programme for training dealers in Europe.

Exports. The company does not export directly. However, it does provide products for projects undertaken in various countries by its clients. These projects are normally initiated via Bamson Company's partnership with Akzo Nobel.

Challenges. Bamson Company's biggest current concern is the use by sprayers of lower segment paint for higher segment cars.

Development agenda. Recent developments include the installation of spray booths or 'ovens' for dealers and private garages, facilitating the fast drying of sprayed cars. About 40 companies have benefited from this scheme. Bamson Company is now planning to widen its product line with the introduction of water-based paints. The company is also positioning itself to introduce protective and marine paints, in response to the commencement of commercial oil production in Ghana. The company has plans to diversify its operations into the hospitality industry as well as into the manufacture of aluminium doors and windows – an area in which its sister company, Glostar, already operates.

14.2.3 PZ Cussons Ghana Limited

Basic details. PZ Cussons Ghana is a publicly traded company listed on the Ghana Stock Exchange. Located in the Tema Heavy Industrial Area on Sanyo Road, the company is a manufacturing and trading company that produces soaps, toiletries, cosmetics, pharmaceuticals, electrical goods and nutritional products. The company began trading in Ghana under the name Paterson Zochonis. In June 2002 the name was changed to PZ Cussons Ghana.

PZ Cussons Ghana employs about 370 workers. The company's turnover was US$38.4 million in 2010.

History. PZ Cussons Ghana is a subsidiary of PZ Cussons PLC, a multinational group incorporated in the UK. The group dates back to 1879 when two young British immigrants named George Henry Paterson and George Zochonis established a trading post in Sierra Leone (Paterson Zochonis) that exported palm oil to Europe.

The company was successful throughout West Africa and in 1934 the firm established a business in what was then known as the Gold Coast (now Ghana). PZ Cussons became a public company in 1976 and was listed on the Ghana Stock Exchange within 12 months of the inception of the exchange in 1990.

From its early activities in importing, exporting and general trading, it went on to set up two industrial bases in 1969 called Sparta Manufacturing Limited and Tema Thread Limited. In the 1980s and 1990s the company changed focus to concentrate on health care products, beauty care products and a wide range of cosmetics and toiletries.

In 1995 the company invested US$10 million in developing a new soap factory to produce high-quality toilet and laundry soap under internationally known brand names such as Imperial Leather and Premier (for toilet soaps) and Canoe and Duck (for laundry soaps).

The name of the group was changed from Paterson Zochonis to PZ Cussons in 2002.

PZ Cussons outsources the production of the over-the-counter pharmaceutical products that it markets. These cover household names such as Drastin, Zubes, Robb, Super Atlas multivitamins and Blood Tonic.

Current activities and products. PZ Cussons Ghana's product range covers personal care, home care, nutrition and electrical products. Under personal care, PZ Cussons produces Venus haircare products, Cussons baby products, Robb medicaments, Imperial Leather powder and medicated mentholated dusting powder. The company also produces Premier, Camel and Imperial Leather toilet soaps. The production of its pharmaceutical products (Zubes, Super Atlas multivitamins and Drastin) has been outsourced since 2010.

Some of the home care brands that the company produces include Camel antiseptics, laundry soaps (Duck Bar soap and Canoe soap) as well as Jet washing powder. Detergents are imported from PZ Cussons Nigeria. Laundry soaps are manufactured in Ghana.

PZ Cussons sells evaporated and powdered milk under the brand name Nunu in the nutrition sector. PZ Cussons Ghana imports these products from Nutricima Nigeria, which is partly owned by PZ Cussons Nigeria.

PZ Cussons has a joint venture with Haier Thermocool of China, under which PZ Cussons distributes and retails Haier Thermocool branded electrical goods including fridges, freezers, washing machines, televisions, DVD players, mobile phones and air conditioning units. (Haier Thermocool has an electrical goods assembly plant in Ghana.)

Organization and management.   PZ Cussons Ghana has a six-member board of directors and a management team comprising 11 functional heads.

Firm capabilities.   PZ Cussons Ghana has substantial production facilities for fast-moving consumer goods and an extensive distribution network. With 80 years' experience of trading in Africa, the company has a wide knowledge of local conditions, enabling it to produce innovative products for the local market.

Competition.   PZ Cussons Ghana's main competitor is Unilever Ghana. It also faces competition across its product range from imported goods from Asia and Europe.

Supply and marketing chain.   Palm kernel oil and palm oil are sourced locally from suppliers. Caustic soda, bleaching earth, antiseptics, turpinol and isopropyl alcohol are imported from Asia (India and China) and Europe.

The company has a network of 30 distribution partners and regional sales offices in Accra, Kumasi, Tamale, Takoradi, Koforidua and Denu.

Exports.   The company exports pharmaceutical products and antiseptic to Nigeria, and laundry soaps to Togo.

14.2.4   BBC Industrial Company (Ghana) Ltd

Basic details.   BBC Industrial Company (Ghana) is a privately owned limited liability company that was established in 1964 to manufacture paints and related products. The company is the largest local paint manufacturer in Ghana and accounts for about 55% of locally produced paints.

BBC has a workforce of 350 of which 300 are permanent employees, the remaining 50 being casuals and contract personnel. The average turnover of the company is in the region of US$45 million per annum.

History. BBC Industrial Company (Ghana) was founded by Boutros BouChedid, a Ghanaian of Lebanese origin, in 1964. Prior to the establishment of the company, BouChedid worked as a contractor. (His projects included the construction of the parliament building.) He also served under the first president of Ghana, Dr Kwame Nkrumah, as Ghana's ambassador to Lebanon.

The company, which started operations in a shed, was owned and managed by BouChedid until 1978, when it was sold to Mohammed Ahmed Odaymat, a Lebanese entrepreneur who was then working with Toyota Ghana. Odaymat has an interest in a number of companies including Rana Motors (the automotive industry), Eakaza Limited (trading in rice, sugar, flour, wheat and cooking oil), Intercom Programming & Manufacturing Company Ghana Limited (an information technology company), Khomara Printing Press Limited, Highland Spring Limited (manufacturers of bottled mineral water) and BBC Industrial Company (Ghana).

When Odaymat took over BBC Industrial Company (Ghana), he developed the Leyland and Leylac brands of paint products. The company has expanded from a single shed to taking up about 80% of the 4-hectare site on which it is located today. The company is currently owned by the Odaymat family.

In the early 1990s Odaymat left the country and his brother-in-law took over the management of the company. Essam Odaymat, a son of Mohammed Ahmed Odaymat, is currently the CEO.

Current activities and products. BBC Industrial Company (Ghana) produces three main products: Leyland branded products, Leylac branded products and Home Charm Emulsion. A fourth product, selling under the brand name Gold, is imported.

Leyland. The company produces several different products under the Leyland brand: cement paint, emulsion, grout, texture paint, tile adhesive, wall putty and white glue.

Leylac. The product line includes alkyd varnish, aluminium silver, anti-rust red oxide, zinc chromate, furniture lacquer and gloss paint, sandy sealer, school board, turpentine, undercoat and wood primer.

Home Charm Emulsion. These are products based on polyvinyl acetate, which gives good performance on interior work. The products are self-priming and produce odourless flat (matt) finishes.

Gold. The company imports seven products for sale under the Gold band: acrylic paint, coloured putty, fungus wash, stabilizing primer, surfacer, texture paint and wall master.

Organization and management. The board comprises the three owners of the company (Mohammed, Rashid and Khodor Odaymat).

An eight-member management team includes the managing director and the deputy managing director, the technical director and five departmental heads (production, quality control, procurement and supply, packaging and loading, and office administration).

Firm capabilities. The factory has a capacity of approximately 30 million litres of paint per annum. Its lines of production include a wide range of specialty paints for industrial applications. Among the new products that it has introduced is the Home Charm range, which is a low-cost line for the high-volume end of the market.

Competition. The main local competitors of the firm are Azar Chemical Industries, Bamson Company and Coral Paints Ghana Limited. The products of BBC Industrial Company (Ghana) also have to compete with a large range of imported paints, including those in the Sikelele and Shield brands.

Supply and marketing chain. Almost all inputs are imported from Europe, Asia and other African countries. The main inputs – calcium carbonate, dryers, pigments, polyvinyl acetate (binder) and oxides – are procured from France, the UK, Egypt, China and India.

The finished products are first sent to the company's warehouse and then delivered to key dealers.

Exports. BBC Industrial Company (Ghana) exports its products to Burkina Faso, Togo and Benin. Although these countries have local paint manufacturing companies, there is a strong market for the products of BBC Industrial Company (Ghana) as a result of their superior quality and robustness. Exports to Nigeria are handled via distributors.

Challenges. The main issues facing the company are the high cost of inputs, especially labour and utilities (electricity).

Development agenda. The main developmental goal of BBC Industrial Company (Ghana) is to maintain its leadership as the largest producer of paints in Ghana. It also aims to become one of the largest producers of oil-based and emulsion paints in the West African subregion.

14.2.5 *Bas van Buuren (BVB) Ghana Limited*

Basic details. BVB was established and registered in Ghana in 2006. Located at Apowa in the Western region of Ghana, it is a Free Zones enterprise that processes coconut husks into organic fertilizer for export.

BVB employs 311 people, including 30 permanent staff, 26 casuals and about 270 contract workers. The contract workers are farmers who grow coconut and supply the husks to the company. BVB has a turnover of over US$500,000 per annum.

History. Bas van Buuren Substrates is a Dutch company established 100 years ago that specializes in greenhouse horticulture, mushroom growing and orchards. BVB Substrates supplies a wide range of substrates to the professional horticultural sector in the Netherlands. The company started as a trade agent for farmers and a supplier of organic fertilizers in the Netherlands and other European countries. BVB Substrates initially imported organic fertilizer from India, Sri Lanka, the Dominican Republic and Ghana.

The Managed Craft Company was established in 1988 by a Ghanaian entrepreneur, Philomena Britain, who at the time processed coconut husks into organic manure for sale to local farmers and to BVB Substrates. Due to the inability of Managed Craft to provide the increasing volumes and quality of husks required by BVB Substrates, and to related operational problems, BVB Substrates took over Managed Craft in 2005, leading to the establishment of Bas van Buuren Ghana Limited the following year.

Current activities and products. BVB produces organic fertilizer from coconut husks.

Organization and management. A three-member board of directors comprises the general manager, the administrative manager and a representative from BVB Substrates. Operations are supervised by a four-member management team.

Firm capabilities. It currently processes nearly a million cubic metres of coconut husks per annum. The company's grinding and pressing facilities enable it to produce quality organic fertilizer.

Competition. BVB's main potential competitor is Wienco Fibre Ghana Limited, a local producer of organic fertilizer. However, as BVB exports all its product to its parent company in the Netherlands, it does not compete directly with Wienco Fibre Ghana in the local market.

Supply and marketing chain. The main input, coconut husks, is procured from contract farmers in the Western region. These contract farmers deliver dry coconut husks that are more than five years old to a collection point, from which they are transported to the factory for drying, grinding and pressing.

Imported inputs such as calcium nitrate are procured locally from importers.

Exports.   BVB Ghana exports all its products to its parent company in the Netherlands.

Challenges.   Access to coconut husks is costly as the growers are widely dispersed and the company has to travel up to 90 km to farms. High energy costs and frequent power outages constitute continuing problems.

Development agenda.   BVB aims to increase its production capacity from the current 350 m^3 every four days to 700 m^3. As part of that process, the company aims to establish its own coconut plantation to improve its supply of coconut husks.

Chapter 15

PLASTICS AND RUBBER

15.1 Sector Profile

Background and overview. The plastics and rubber industries cover tyre manufacturing, plastic products, electrical materials, motor vehicle equipment, rubber hoses, glass and plastic packaging. Plastic packaging products include consumer products and prescription containers, fibreglass and composite materials, plastic compounds and resins, and household products.

There is no strong link between the two industries in Ghana. The rubber industry is basically involved in the development of rubber plantations and the harvesting and export of raw rubber. The plastics industry imports all its inputs.

As of 2009 there were two rubber plantations, covering a total area of 11,255 hectares between them. Figures produced by the Ministry of Food and Agriculture show that the volume of natural rubber produced increased from 13,619 mt in 2006 to 15,318 mt in 2007, before decreasing to 14,132 mt in 2008. The decline in production in 2008 was attributed to the replacement and replanting of old trees by Ghana Rubber Estates Limited, the owners of the main rubber plantation in Ghana. Production recovered to 16,000 mt in 2009. The sector provides employment for 37,083 farmers through its outgrower scheme.[1]

The plastics industry produces polymer materials and intermediate products for the building and construction industry, the electronics industry, the chemicals industry, the packaging industry and the transportation industry. The growing demand for consumer products, processed foods, beverages and food delivery services has created a strong market for plastic packaging in Ghana. The growth of the construction sector drives the growing demand for PVC pipes.

[1] Under the Outgrower Plantation Scheme, an estimated 8,100 farmers will be organized into outgrower schemes through which support and other assistance from bigger rubber estate developers will be channelled. The developers will provide a mechanism for input distribution, mobilization of the producers and a market outlet for the farmers' output.

The plastics subsector employs 150,000 people in 895 plastic manufacturing companies, producing around 26,000 mt of assorted plastic products annually. About 70% of the plastics companies are located in or close to Accra.

Structure of the plastics industry. The plastics industry comprises three segments.

(i) **Pipes.** The manufacture of PVC and high-density polyethylene (HDPE) pipes constitutes by far the largest segment of the plastics industry. PVC pipes are widely used in potable water supply and distribution, electrical installations, telecommunication, irrigation, bore-hole drilling, sewerage and drainage systems, among other things. The leading companies in this segment are Interplast Limited, Duraplast Ghana Limited and Top Industries Ghana Limited.

(ii) **Household plastic wares.** Household plastic wares include chairs, bowls, plates, cups, spoons and buckets. There are currently two major companies in the subsector, along with several medium- and small-scale enterprises involved in retailing. These products compete against a substantial flow of imports, especially from China.

(iii) **Plastic sachets, bottles and packaging.** This segment of the industry provides domestic beverage and bottled water manufacturers with about 60% of their plastic containers. Other products include expandable polystyrene products that are used as containers for consumer goods.

Supply and marketing chain.

Rubber. Tapped rubber from trees is collected and stored in containers. The raw rubber is then processed into sheets and packed for sale. In the rubber commodity markets, producers generally rely on dealers and brokers, but in Ghana the two main rubber producers have established direct links to customers. The two companies also contract to buy the products produced by small producers (outgrowers) to augment their supplies.

Plastics. The main inputs are plastic granules, metal sheets/rolls, paper master rolls, film master rolls and various chemicals, all of which are imported from China, India, South East Asia and the Middle East. The PVC and HDPE manufacturers (Interplast Limited, the Poly Group of Companies and Qualiplast) export large volumes of their products to Togo, Benin, Nigeria, Niger, Mali, Angola, Sierra Leone, Liberia, Burkina Faso, Chad, Cameroon, Ivory Coast, Cameroon, Senegal, Equatorial Guinea, Gambia, Guinea Bissau and Mauritania.

Ghana exports substantial volumes of packaging materials to other countries in West Africa.

Policy context. The Ministry of Food and Agriculture commissioned a Rubber Master Plan study in 2001. The study proposed an output target of 50,000 mt of rubber by 2020 and forecast a growth in world rubber demand of 3% per annum to 2020 and a rise in rubber prices from a level of US$0.60/kg in 2003 to about US$2.50/kg in 2020.[2] This provided the background for the government's support of the subsector.

With a target of achieving export earnings of US$50 million by 2017, the government is lending support to small farmers through credit schemes and making available more land for the cultivation of rubber. The government is also promoting high-yielding and disease-resistant clones of rubber as well as installing new processing facilities and providing training to rubber producers.

In plastics, the current import tax regime, which imposes a tax of almost 40% on imported products, is designed to protect the local industry from cheaper imported plastic products from China and elsewhere.

A second focus of policy relates to the problem of disposal of plastic waste. A 2010 measure imposed a tax on sachet water producers to fund an initiative in this area.

Challenges. The rubber sector of Ghana has stagnated since the closure of Bonsa Tyre Company Limited in 2000. Bonsa Tyre was the only tyre factory in Ghana and it provided a ready market for natural rubber.[3] The total area under cultivation has remained at roughly the same level for over a decade.

The main issues facing the plastics industry relate to competition from imported products. Operators consider the taxation regime to be disadvantageous to local manufacturers: while raw materials attract an import duty of 10%, imported finished products attract duty of 40%, rendering locally manufactured rubber products uncompetitive compared with imported products.[4]

Waste management disposal methods and recycling have been the subject of recent debates among stakeholders.

Export status, strength and potential. About 95% of the country's rubber output is currently exported to France, Turkey, East Africa and South Korea.

---

[2] Khumbanyiwa, A. G. 2001. *Smallholder Agroforestry (Rubber) Project.* Report, African Development Bank.

[3] Bonsa Tyre has been placed on divestiture by the Divesture Implementation Committee.

[4] *Business News*, October 2006, Article 113075. Ghana Web.

The export destinations of PVC and HDPE products have already been noted. The exported products include packaging crates for breweries in Nigeria, Sierra Leone, Cameroon, Liberia and Kenya.

Ghana is also a leading producer and exporter of packaging materials (such as expandable polystyrene boxes) for fresh fish, fruits and vegetables. Ghana ranks second to Nigeria in the regional export of packaging materials, with an export value of US$300 million in 2006.[5] Ghana is also the second largest exporter of polyethylene terephthalate (PET) bottles in the subregion.

Recent developments. An important recent development is the increase in income of rubber plantation farmers in the Western and Central regions following the signing of an agreement between Ghana, Germany and France in 2008. Under the agreement, each farmer is expected to earn US$5,294 per year for a 4 hectare farm. This is expected to yield US$24.3 million for the country from the production of 16,500 mt of rubber annually.[6]

Under the Trade Sector Support Programme of the PSI on Rubber, a recent study was conducted to review the effects of tariffs on industrial concerns. This study will inform the Ministry of Trade and Industry in guiding policy.

A medium-sized company. In the next section we profile four of the largest firms: Interplast Limited and Qualiplast Limited in plastics, and Ghana Rubber Estates Limited and Latex Foam Rubber Products Limited in rubber. Here, we look at a typical medium-sized firm, Strong Plast Limited.

Strong Plast is a family-owned private company that produces household plastic wares for the domestic market. The company employs 65 workers.

Strong Plast was established by Tony Saoud, a Ghanaian entrepreneur, in 1996. The company commenced operations with one plant and produced 10,000 units of plastic products per month. Prior to establishing the company, Saoud had interests in other businesses and his companies produce between 40,000 and 45,000 units of plastic products per month. These include plastic chairs, tables, basins, baskets, buckets and crates. The company produces more than 20 different types of household product. Churches are among its main clients.

The company guarantees its products for a minimum of two years. Various distributors sell its products in neighbouring countries. The firm's current plan is to extend its reach throughout the country, and especially in the Northern region.

---

[5] *Enterprise Competitiveness.* International Trade Centre Report, 25 March 2009.
[6] Ghana News Agency report, August 2006.

Rationale for selecting profiled firms. Interplast Limited is the largest manufacturer of PVC and HDPE pipes in West Africa. Qualiplast Limited is the largest manufacturer of assorted plastic wares. Ghana Rubber Estates Limited is the oldest and largest producer of rubber. Latex Foam Rubber Products Limited is the largest foam factory.

15.2   Profiles of Major Firms

15.2.1   Interplast Limited

Basic details. Interplast is a limited liability company incorporated under the Companies Code of 1963 (Act 179). The company is one of the largest manufacturing firms in Ghana and is one of the biggest producers of plastic pipe systems and fittings in West Africa. The company operates under three brand names: Interplast for pipes and fittings; Everlast for reinforced unplasticized polyvinyl chloride (uPVC) doors, windows and profiles; and Panelast for wall and ceiling panels.

Interplast employs over 600 people and had a turnover of over US$50 million per annum in 2010.

History. Interplast is a wholly owned Ghanaian company founded in 1970 by Saied Fakhry, a Lebanese national who immigrated to Ghana. Prior to setting up the company, Fakhry was a trader of general merchandise in Ghana. The company is privately owned by the Fakhry family. Fakhry has been the chairman of the company since its foundation and his son, Hayssam Fakhry, is currently the managing director.

Current activities and products. Interplast produces a wide range of plastic pipes and related products. The company meets most of Ghana's requirements for small- and large-diameter PVC pipes for water supply throughout the country. Interplast is one of the largest manufacturers of plastic pipes in the whole of West Africa. Its products include pipes and fittings, specially designed and fabricated silicone-coated pipes, cable protection pipes, field underground drainage solutions, soil and waste systems, wall and ceiling panels, and reinforced uPVC doors and windows. Specific products include

- HDPE drip irrigation pipes,
- HDPE pressure pipes,
- uPVC conduits,
- polypropylene random piping systems,

- uPVC borehole pipes,
- cable duct systems,
- HDPE hand-crafted fittings,
- sewer systems,
- wall and ceiling panels and
- Terrazzo Divider Stripes (for floor and wall dividing).

Interplast manufactures uPVC pipes to British Standard BS 3505 and DIN 8062 specifications and HDPE pipes to DIN 8074-75 and ISO 4422-2 specifications. All pipes are tested and certified by the Ghana Standards Board.

Interplast sells to several sectors including the water, mining, oil and gas, agriculture, telecommunications, construction and civil engineering, aviation and electricity industries.

Interplast also provides welding services, undertakes installation and provides general training.

Organization and management. Interplast has a three-member board comprising the chairman, the managing director and a CEO (Arthur Huberts). Functional heads are responsible for production, administration, finance and marketing.

Firm capabilities. Interplast produces products to international quality standards and is certified to ISO 9001. The firm's laboratory tests every production batch and is able to provide clients with an EN 10204:2005–3.1 inspection certificate.

The company has upgraded its production capacity to enable it to produce polyethylene pipes up to 1,000 mm in diameter. In 2011 the company introduced seven new products: warning mesh, barrier mesh, HDPE gas pipes, mosquito nets, iron rebar clips, Interplast super strength pipes and polyethylene/polypropylene pipes.

The company offers customized solutions and products for major infrastructure projects.

Competition. The main competitors of Interplast are Duraplast, Top Industries, the Poly Group of Companies and Pipes and Plastics Products Limited, each of which has a product range that overlaps with that of Interplast in some areas.

Supply and marketing chain. The main inputs of the company – such as PVC compound, plasticizers, stabilizers, colour pigments, fire retardants, protective materials and other filling materials – are imported from Europe and the US.

Interplast sells directly to the retail market as well as supplying businesses and the government directly.

Exports. Interplast currently exports to Togo, Benin, Nigeria, Niger, Mali, Angola, Sierra Leone, Liberia, Burkina Faso, Chad, Cameroon, Ivory Coast, Cameroon, Senegal, Equatorial Guinea, Gambia, Guinea Bissau and Mauritania.

Challenges. The main current concern for the company is the high cost of energy.

Development agenda. The long-term goal of the company is to maintain its quality standards and to expand its role as West Africa's leading producer of plastic pipe systems.

15.2.2 Qualiplast Limited

Basic details. Qualiplast was incorporated as a limited liability company in 1973 to manufacture and supply industrial packaging containers and household plastic wares to both local and international markets.

Qualiplast is part of the Hitti Group of companies, which also includes Duraplast (a manufacturer of uPVC, PVC and HDPE pipes and fittings) and Ashfoam Company Limited (a manufacturer of foam products), all of which are located in Ghana. In addition to its businesses in Ghana, the group owns Promousse in Niger and Benin and Duraplast in Niger.

The company has 500 employees and its annual turnover lies between US$1.8 million and US$2.5 million.

History. Qualiplast started as a small factory with the name Greenplastica Limited in 1973. Set up by Robert Hitti as a family business, the company started with one small depot and equipment that gave it an operating capacity of between 50 mt and 100 mt per month. With a total of 60 employees, its annual turnover fluctuated between US$200,000 and US$300,000 in the early years. The name of the company was changed to Qualiplast in 1992.

Qualiplast currently produces between 6,840 mt and 7,800 mt of products per annum. Operations on a second site, at Tema, were closed down in 2000 to concentrate activities at the Accra location. Qualiplast also now has four depots across the country.

The company has won various awards from local and international organizations, including the World Packaging Organization (2005), the Ghana Export Promotion Council (2004) and the Foundation for Excellence in Business Practice (2003).

Current activities and products.   Qualiplast manufactures three product lines: (a) crates for beverages; (b) industrial containers for packaging; and (c) household products.

The company's 1,500 products include basins, baskets, bottles, bowls and buckets, dustbins, funnels, ice cream containers, jars, jerrycans, jugs and mugs, paint gallons, plates, spoons, tablet containers, tea kettles, trays, tumblers, toys, water bottles and crates.

Qualiplast's plastic packaging products serve various industries: cosmetics, chemicals, pharmaceuticals, breweries and foods and beverages.

Organization and management.   Reporting to the board of the group are the managing directors of the various constituent companies. Qualiplast has four divisions: production and engineering, finance and administration, marketing, and research and development.

The Hitti Group remains a family firm with a family member heading each operation. The managing directors of Qualiplast and Duraplast are both relatives of Robert Hitti. Robert Hitti's eldest son heads Ashfoam Company Limited.

Firm capabilities.   The company has a state-of-the-art plant and more than 150 types of equipment and moulds, as well as a strong team of engineers, chemists, technicians and operators. Its international network allows it to source any type of complex mould.

Supply and marketing chain.   Raw materials are mainly imported from Brazil, the US and Saudi Arabia.

The company uses distributors to reach its clients, who include Coca Cola Bottling Company Ghana, Guinness Ghana Breweries, Accra Breweries, Ghana Rubber Estates Limited, Unilever Ghana Limited, Total, Shell, Ghana Oil Company, Cocoa Processing Company Limited, Ernest Chemists and Ayrton Drugs.

Exports.   Qualiplast's products are exported to Liberia, Ivory Coast, Benin, Nigeria, Mali, Congo, Guinea, Guinea Bissau, Senegal, Gambia, Togo, Angola and Kenya. Clients include Guinness Nigeria and Guinness Cameroon, Coca Cola Sierra Leone (Freetown Cold Storage), Sierra Leone Breweries Ltd, Monrovia Breweries Inc. (Liberia), Coca Cola Liberia (United

States Trading Company), and East Africa Industries of Kenya. The company also exports to Europe and South America.

Development agenda. In the medium term, Qualiplast is aiming to become the first producer of plastic pallets in Ghana – driving the replacement of wood products with plastic products – and to focus on large-size/value products.

15.2.3 *Ghana Rubber Estates Limited (GREL)*

Basic details. GREL is a limited liability company established in 1957. With its headquarters in Takoradi and field operations in the Ahanta West district of the Western region, the company has the largest industrial rubber plantation in Ghana. Some 60% of its shares are owned by Société Internationale De Plantations D'Hévéas (SIPH), a French company, with the government of Ghana owning 25% and the remaining 15% being owned by Newgen Limited, a Ghanaian company.

GREL employs 350 permanent workers, 2,000 direct contract workers (mainly tappers) and over 3,000 indirect contract workers who are responsible for the slashing and budding of the plantations. The annual turnover of the company was US$41.2 million in 2010.

History. GREL was established in 1957 by R. T. Briscoe, a Ghanaian entrepreneur, at Dixcove in the Western region. Prior to setting up the company, Briscoe owned a timber and wood processing company. The company started as a small private enterprise with a plantation size of 923 hectares. The plantation was nationalized in 1960 through the Agricultural Development Corporation and, in 1962, became part of the State Farms Corporation. By that time, the plantation had been expanded to three locations: Dixcove, Abura and Subri, all in the Western region.

The government established a joint venture company in 1967 with the Firestone Tyre Company of the US to take over the rubber plantation. The joint venture company, named Ghana Rubber Estates Limited, inherited a plantation of 39,390 hectares.

In 1990 Firestone sold its shares in GREL to the government of Ghana and the company became a wholly state-owned entity. After that the government of Ghana entered into a financing agreement with Caisse Française de Développement (now Agence Française de Développement) to develop and manage the rubber plantation and to build a new rubber processing plant at Apimenim, in the Western region, in 1995–96. In 1996 the French management company SIPH became the major shareholder.

Current activities and products. GREL is involved in the planting of rubber trees and the processing and marketing of rubber. The company processes cup lumps into crumb rubber at its factory located at Apimenim in the Ahanta West district in the Western region of Ghana.

Organization and management. GREL has a five-member board comprising the managing director, two members from SIPH, and one representative each from the government of Ghana and from Newgen Limited. The company has a 14-member senior management team that includes the managing director and the functional heads.

Firm capabilities. GREL processes 14,704 mt of cup lumps into crumb rubber annually. The company meets the technical requirements of leading global rubber companies.

Competition. GREL has a domestic monopoly in the production of rubber. A number of firms are known to be considering entry to the industry.

Supply and marketing chain. In addition to rubber harvested from its own plantations, GREL receives cup lumps supplies from numerous individual outgrowers. Output is transported some 30 km to the nearby port using the company's own vehicles as well as third-party truckers.

Under the management agreement between the government and Agence Française de Développement, SIPH is responsible for marketing all the rubber produced by the company.

Exports. GREL exports about 96% of its output to the European and Asian markets. A single customer, Michelin, accounts for 70%.

Challenges. The key issues facing GREL include difficulties in securing additional land for expanding its plantations at their current locations, the rising cost of labour, the high cost of utilities and the fluctuating price of rubber on the international market.

Development agenda. GREL aims to expand its operation and increase its processing capacity from the current 14,704 mt per annum to 22,000 mt in 2015 and then to 37,000 mt in 2020.

15.2.4 Latex Foam Rubber Products Limited

Basic details. Latex Foam Rubber Products is a family business established in 1969. Located in the North Industrial Area in Accra, Latex Foam Rubber Products is Ghana's oldest foam manufacturing company and is the largest in the industry.

The company has a staff strength of over 500 and had an annual turnover of US$22 million in 2010.

History.   Latex Foam Rubber Products was started in 1969 by two siblings: Aid Solomon Laba and Nowfill Solomon Laba, both Ghanaians of Lebanese origin. Prior to the establishment of Latex Foam Rubber Products, Aid and Nowfill traded in general merchandise. They also had business interests in pipes, plastics and information technology and established the companies Pipes and Plastic Products Limited and Moonbeam.

Latex Foam Rubber Products entered the market using the Dunlop Technology under license from the Dunlop Company. The technology gave Latex Foam Rubber Products a quality advantage in the rather traditional market of that time. In 1972 the company started the production of spring interior mattresses.[7] In 1974 production capacity was increased to 300 spring mattresses a day. The company introduced high-density foam mattresses and super-soft foam for furniture upholstery in 1992 and reinforced spring mattresses and sofa beds in 1994. In 1996 the company established another factory in Kumasi as well as depots in all the regional capitals in Ghana. The company also introduced several types of pillow, including back care pillows, cushions and leg rests. Latex Foam Rubber Products established two factories in Niger and Burkina Faso in 2001 and 2002, respectively. Its pocketed-spring and nested-spring products were introduced onto the market in 2006 and the company was the first to produce such products in West Africa. Latex Foam Rubber Products became the first to produce high resilient foam mattresses in the Ghanaian market in 2007 with the introduction of its Ultraflex mattress. The company introduced an anti-stress mattress in 2010 and it was the first company in West Africa to produce viscoelastic (memory) foam mattresses. The company was awarded the International Arch of Europe Award for quality in Frankfurt, Germany in 2010.

Current activities and products.   Latex Foam Rubber Products manufactures eight product lines: spring mattresses, foam mattresses, upholstery, student mattresses, sofa beds, pillows, therapeutic products and beds.

Organization and management.   Latex Foam Rubber Products has a five-member board and a management team comprising the managing director, the general manager, the assistant general manager and the line managers.

---

[7] Both the interior production and the assembly of the unit springs for the mattresses were done at the factory premises.

Firm capabilities. Latex Foam Rubber Products was the first firm to produce several different types of foam product in Ghana: these include its honeymoon mattress (the most popular mattress in Ghana and West Africa), its anti-stress mattress and its viscoelastic (memory) foam mattress. Its production facilities were rebuilt following a serious fire in 2007 and are now state of the art.

Competition. The local competitors of Latex Foam Rubber Products are Ashfoam and Nsawam Foam. There is also competition from imported foams and mattresses from Europe and the US.

Supply and marketing chain. The key inputs – TDI Polyol, methylene chloride, Jacquard clothing and polyester – are imported, mainly from Europe and China. The company sources rubber (polythene) and thread through local suppliers who import them.

Exports. The company exports to Togo, Ivory Coast, Mali and Benin.

Challenges. The main issues facing Latex Foam Rubber Products are the high cost of raw materials and utilities. High interest rates are also a continuing problem. Delays in the delivery of (imported) inputs sometime delay production.

Development agenda. Latex Foam Rubber Products currently aims to expand its production capacity with a view to increasing sales, both domestically and in its export markets.

IGC International Growth Centre

The International Growth Centre aims to promote sustainable growth in developing countries by providing demand-led policy advice based on frontier research. Based at London School of Economics (LSE) and in partnership with Oxford University, the IGC is initiated and funded by the UK Department for International Development.

The IGC has active country programmes in Bangladesh, Ethiopia, Ghana, India (Central and Bihar), Mozambique, Pakistan, Rwanda, Sierra Leone, Tanzania and Zambia and supports over 200 individual research projects on issues of governance, human capital, agriculture, infrastructure, trade, firm capabilities, state capacity, macroeconomics, finance and climate change.

The IGC is directed by a Steering Group that consists of two Academic Directors – one from the London School of Economics and one from Oxford University – as well as leading academics from prestigious British and American universities.

Contact us:

International Growth Centre
London School of Economics and Political Science
4th Floor
Tower Two
Houghton Street
London WC2A 2AE
United Kingdom

www.theigc.org

+44 (0)20 7955 6144

For all enquiries, please contact
Mazida Khatun: mazida.khatun@theigc.org